Nature Study Hacking

Weather, Wind & Water

Created by Joy Cherrick

Copyright © 2019 Joy Cherrick
All rights reserved.
ISBN-10: 1693020964
ISBN-13: 978-1693020964

All designed and formatted by Joy Cherrick
Images of credit: Canva.com

This publication is a creative work protected in full by all applicable copyright laws, as well as by misappropriation, trade secret, unfair competition and other applicable laws. No part of this book may be reproduced or transmitted in any manner without permission from Joy Cherrick, except in the case of brief quotations embodied in critical articles or reviews. All rights reserved.

Introduction to Nature Study	6
Introduction to Weather| Lesson 1	27
Vocabulary- Climate vs Weather| Lesson 2	28
Experiment - Evaporation| Lesson 3	29
Perpetual Journal Entry| Lesson 4	29
Intro to the Earth's Atmosphere| Lesson 5	31
Diagram of the earth's atmosphere| Lesson 6	32
Winds | Lesson 7	34
Review, Improve & Delight| Lesson 8	35
Poem| Lesson 9	36
Cloud Watching| Lesson 10	37
Clouds - Read and Watch | Lesson 11	38
Cloud Types Diagram | Lesson 12	39
Review, Improve & Delight| Lesson 13	40
Telling the weather| Lesson 14	42
Telling the weather continued| Lesson 15	43
Poem| Lesson 16	44
Snow and Ice - Demonstration| Lesson 17	45
Snow and Ice Continued| Lesson 18	46
Perpetual Journal Entry| Lesson 19	47
Rain and Lightning| Lesson 20	48
Rain and Lightning Continued| Lesson 21	49
Rainbow Experiment| Lesson 22	50
Draw a Rainbow | Lesson 23	51
Perpetual Journal Entry| Lesson 24	52
Weather| Exam Week	54
Poems about Weather	55
Resources	56

Thanks to Kevin for taking the kids to the aquarium and
picking up the groceries so I could write.

Thanks also, Cindy, Jeannette, Joyce and Rochelle for inspiring me, supporting me and humoring me.
This series is a result of friendship.

Finally, thanks to my mom for editing, watching kids and telling me to "go for it."

Introduction to Nature Study

"The child must not be left to discover everything for himself;
his mind must be prepared in some measure for what he is to see and observe.
It has been well said that the previous history of the mind
determines the impression which the sight of any object is to make.
"We can only see what we have been trained to see."
The Parents' Review, *"How to Best Study Nature"* by Mr. J. C. Medd, M.A.

When I started my homeschooling journey sometime around 2009 or 2010, my mom sent me copies of *For the Family's Sake* and *For the Children's Sake* by Susan Schaeffer Macaulay. It was through these books that I discovered and adopted the philosophy of Charlotte Mason. Mason's ideas about educating a whole person were like a soothing balm to my soul. How did I miss that true learning involves the things that I find engaging in the world? Why had I fallen into the trap of chasing academics alone? I am so grateful and forever indebted to the unmarried school teacher, Charlotte Mason. Her life's work was to be a student of the ways of children, watch how they learn, seek out the very best for them and then, share what she learned.

The study of nature is one of the habits that sets apart the Charlotte Mason method from other literature-based or classical educational philosophies. I have done my best to get my children out-of-doors (as Mason puts it) with great regularity. We have lived most of our parenthood in subdivided neighborhoods with two glorious years spent in a farmhouse and then in a house in the woods. I know that it is much easier to get outside and explore nature when there is a generous feast just beyond the kitchen window calling to me. We are once again living in a subdivision, and I've had to develop some tools to help me continue getting our children introduced to nature so that they too will be able to call the trees, flowers and birds by name so that they will know they are friends.

As a small child, my family spent two years living on one acre squished between a herd of cattle beyond one fence and a circus horse and pony on the other. It was in this home that I was able to see my first bird's nest and chrysalis, and I became intimately acquainted with the daffodil, which remains my favorite flower to this day. I'm sure I watched some Sesame Street while living there, but my most vivid memories are of my time spent exploring our country acre.

During times of stress, loneliness and upheaval, I've always found restoration and solace in nature - be it animals, birds, trees or flowers. They seem to remind me of God's unchanging stability. They help me remember how small I am and how vast God is. Such comfort and joy. I credit much of this love and intimacy with nature to my mother's love of it herself and getting to spend unscheduled time out in it as a young child.
As Anna Comstock poetically describes in Handbook of Nature Study:

"Nature-study cultivates in the child a love of the beautiful; it brings to him early a perception of color, form, and music. He sees whatever there is in his environment, whether it be the thunder-head piled up in the western sky, or the golden flash of the oriole in the elm; whether it be the purple of the shadows on the snow, or the azure glint on the wing of the little butterfly. Also, what there is of sound, he hears; he reads the music score of the bird orchestra, separating each part and knowing which bird sings it. And the pattern of the rain, the gurgle of the brook, the sighing of the wind in the pine, he notes and loves and becomes enriched thereby."

And we all sigh collectively and agree, that YES, this is what we want to learn to sense, experience and even express if it is in our ability to do so. Even if we have just a small bit of this level of love and intimacy with nature, we and our children will be certainly closer to what God created us as humans to be and experience from life.

So, what is nature study exactly? Why is it worth interrupting my school day in order to be sure it gets done? How should I get started? What is involved? Do I really have to read about the subjects we are studying each term? Why should I plan out our nature studies? Can't I just learn about things as we go?

Let's explore these questions and see if we can find a few helpful answers. I'm certainly not a nature study expert. But, I am passionate about introducing children and their grown-ups to nature. I also enjoy finding ways to make things simple so that I will actually do them. "A goal without a plan is just a wish," penned French writer Antoine de Saint-Exupery. So, if nature study is your goal, I will reveal a modest plan to help you and your children not only begin studying nature together, but also start a nature journal and hopefully, make the study of nature a habit that you and your children will make your own and enjoy freely. That is what has happened in our home, and it is my prayer that it will happen in yours!

The world is so full of a number of things, I'm sure we should all be as happy as kings.
\- Robert Louis Stevenson

Nature Study Defined

Through him all things were made;
without him nothing was made that has been made.
John 1:3

What Nature Study is and what it is not is important to determine before we go on.

na·ture
/ˈnāCHər/
Noun
the phenomena of the physical world collectively, including plants, animals, the landscape, and other features and products of the earth, as opposed to humans or human creations.

So "nature study" is the study of the physical world collectively or the study of all things visible created by God. We use our senses when we study nature. We don't break apart, analyze or deconstruct, we observe the whole so that we may know it. Here's a helpful definition:

"Nature Study, as a process, **is seeing the things that one looks at, and the drawing of proper conclusions from what one sees.** Its purpose is to educate the child in terms of his environment, to the end *that his life may be fuller and richer*. Nature Study is not the study of a science, as of botany, entomology, geology, and the like. That is, it takes the things at hand and endeavors to understand them, without reference primarily to the systematic order or relationships of objects. It is informal, as are the objects which one sees. It is entirely divorced from mere definitions, or from formal explanations in books. It is therefore supremely natural. **It trains the eye and the mind to see and to comprehend the common things of life; and the result is not directly the acquiring of science but the establishing of a living sympathy with everything that is.**" (Emphasis mine.)
From "*Leaflet I: What Is Nature-Study?*" written by Liberty Hyde Bailey.

And so I am treading carefully when I attempt to provide a guide for mothers to better lead children into the joys of Nature Study. The spontaneity and "supremely natural" aspects of nature study are helpful to keep in mind as we try to get a handle on the practical habits we need to form to:

1. Take our children out regularly for the purpose of Nature Study

2. Decide what do we do while we are out there

3. Figure out how to actually use those charming Nature Journals without ending up frustrated and annoyed at our little darlings.

All of this, can be accomplished with less resistance if the children are following the lead of a mother who is herself seeking to learn. In fact, Nature Study is one of the areas in family life where the children and the parents can be co-learners. There has been many a time when my children notice, recognize or name something we've discovered where I am in complete ignorance. It is truly satisfying once this happens because you know that they are starting to take the responsibility of self-education. In this co-learning role, a mother can lead with her enthusiasm and wonder. Such as simply asking "I wonder where that squirrel lives?" or "I wonder why those caterpillars are all crossing the road together?" These questions may be difficult to find on Google, but I am always surprised at how much not knowing encourages deeper learning. As Anna Comstock (*Handbook of Nature Study*) put it "the object of the nature-study teacher should be to cultivate in the children powers of accurate observation and to build up within them understanding."

Now that we've explored what Nature Study is, it is important to look more closely at "WHY" we should include it in a STEM/STEAM world. You might ask, "can't they just google it and find out what something is?" or perhaps you think there is not a utilitarian purpose for Nature Study as in "what can they DO to earn money with this information?"

In a world where truth is always being muddled and manipulated, it is important for our children to encounter truth as a matter of habit. For the child, Comstock tells us, "Nature Study cultivates in him a perception and a regard for what is true, and the power to express it. All things seem possible in nature; yet this seeming is always guarded by the eager quest of what is true. Perhaps half the falsehood in the world is due to lack of power to detect the truth and to express it. Nature study aids both in discernment and in expression of things as they are."

When our family is able to learn about The Way Things Are together and does so as a regular rhythm of our family life, then we are getting the opportunity to experience and talk about the little things that truly matter with our children. There is so much in nature that can teach us lessons about getting along with others, death, procreation, colors, war, peace, beauty, weather, truth etc. All of these are available lessons if we are willing take the time to pay attention.

Another way that the study of nature is valuable is that it has been the inspiration for arts, music and dance. All throughout recorded history, we find the relationship with mankind and nature reveals our need of it and closeness to it. Of course our food source comes from nature. And our lives are forever entwined with it even though we seem more separated from the inconveniences of nature. We also miss out on becoming intimately familiar with its ebbs and flows unless we take the time to be outside regularly.

The reality is, we could live all our lives never encountering nature at all. You could stay inside your home all day and when you leave from your garage, head to a store or church and walk inside never touching the soles of your shoes to dirt. On the days that I don't get outside for one reason or another, I know that I missed something. I certainly missed the sunrise or sunset, but I also missed the birds playing or the squirrels jumping through the trees. I may have missed the flowers bloom and fade. All this is nothing I think about or even think I miss. But for some reason if I take time to pursue those little moments, my day is better. It makes me feel smaller or more poetic. Sometimes I feel that I'm getting to witness God at work in the midst of a mundane day.

Perhaps the most important reason to develop the habit of studying nature is to cultivate wonder and learn more about God. We can learn about God's attention to detail when making the tiny ant. Or what about His creativity when making insects that engage in metamorphosis and change from one type of creature to another? We can also learn about God's love for His creation as we learn about how He has equipped us for work. "Look at the birds of the air," we read, "they neither sow nor reap nor gather into barns, and yet your heavenly Father feeds them." (Matthew 6:26) Surely we are of more value than these. We can also simply sit in awe of God by watching a sunset or listening to the waves breaking on the shore. He is great and we are small. We are weak and He is strong. All of these old lofty ideas become intimate truths we claim and agree with as we learn more about the world He created for us to live in, work in and learn about Him through.

> *"But ask the animals, and they will teach you,*
> *or the birds in the sky, and they will tell you;*
> *or speak to the earth, and it will teach you,*
> *or let the fish in the sea inform you.*
> *Which of all these does not know that the hand of the LORD has done this?*
> *In his hand is the life of every creature and the breath of all mankind."*
> Job 12:7-10

Roles

I will be a lion
And you shall be a bear,
And each of us will have a den
Beneath a nursery chair;
And you must growl and growl and growl,
And I will roar and roar,
And then--why, then--you'll growl again,
And I will roar some more!
Wild Beasts, by Evaleen Stein, 1863-1923
from *Child Songs of Cheer*, 1918

Mother's Role in Nature Study

Mother as a Guide

When I first began trying to figure out just exactly HOW to do Nature Study with my children, I heard mothers say to do it casually: "just do it when you are outside with your children" or "it will just happen as you go." Well, friends, that NEVER happened. I was always wrangling or distracted by one thing or another. In addition, it's too overwhelming to go out into The Wide World without a plan.

You need a plan.

Your plan will begin with one topic to look for when you go out. Trees? Birds? Wildflowers? Clouds? Weather? **Pick ONE!** You may want to get all fancy and add a subcategory. Don't do that, not at first. You need to actually get STARTED studying nature, and choosing ONE topic to study will help you get focused and have a sense of purpose to your time spent in nature. This is especially true if you are new to a region or new to learning to call things by name.

Once you choose your topic, say "trees," you will notice how many trees in your neighborhood that you can't name. That is ok! In fact, that means you are on the right track. Humility is essential to learning. From here, you will want to read a little bit about the topic you selected. (If you can't find time, then find a book you will read to your children

ABOUT your topic so that you can all begin learning about it together.) The absolute best place for a mother to start is to read the section in _Handbook of Nature Study_ on the topic you've selected. This may take two or three sittings (remember you are only reading about ONE TOPIC (don't get overwhelmed thinking that you have to read the whole tome!)), but it is full of worthy information that will help you talk with your children about how trees live and grow and how trees differ from one another etc.

If you only have time to read to your child to learn about trees, I recommend _The Tree Book for Kids and Their Grownups._ This book will explain how a tree eats, what photosynthesis is, and it also has some delightful stories about some of the more common North American Trees. As you read to your children, it is really best if you only read one or two pages from this book at a time. This is because they introduce new concepts and explain some of the scientific terms. Sometimes that's cool and sometimes nobody but mother cares. This too is just fine. Your education matters too! You can take some of this new knowledge on the road with you.

With your book learning under your belt, it is now time to go outside WITH your children. Charlotte Mason emphasizes this in Home Education, and I know that sometimes it is easy to ignore this as "charming" or "idealistic." But, going out into nature with your children is not JUST good for them. _It is good for you too, and it is good for your relationship with them._ I enjoy taking a daily walk with my children. We don't go far, just around our block. But this little habit has brought so much restoration and healing to us and has saved many days.

Let's review:
1. Pick the ONE topic you are going to study this term or year.
2. Read up a little about this topic so that you get acquainted with basic terms and categories. You can focus on how it eats and reproduces.
3. Go outside WITH your children.

Now that you are outside with your children, let's talk about your attitude. Are you dressed properly for the weather? If you are going into the woods, are you wearing the proper shoes so that you aren't squeamish about meeting various wild creatures? We all have varying levels of comfort here, so let's assume you are walking on a sidewalk in your suburban hood. Please be dressed comfortably for the weather and elements you will face. (If you need more outerwear, I've had good luck just asking friends if they have unused things like raincoats or umbrellas. Even rain boots and snow gear can be easily found at thrift shops or online consignment for great prices. This is an investment in your family. If you have the right gear, you will find a way for your children to get the right gear as well).

Attire is the first step, but you will also need to remember that you are a co-learner with your children. Your wonder and curiosity will rub off on them, if it's genuine. I think that a simple desire to learn is all that is required.

Please do not be a stick-in-the-mud or have a grumpy attitude for the entire outing. Set your expectations ahead of time. Let them know how to meet them. And, if they are very young or very new to exploring, then it may be helpful to spend the first five minutes practicing your guidelines. (For instance, they may not cross the street without you. Or no running ahead where they can't be seen. Or, you may need to let them know that they are not allowed to play in the creek during this trip because you are in the middle of the school day and they will be free to come back after lessons. etc.) This is basic classroom management, but when it's our own children, it's very easy to forget that we need to tell them what we expect of them and then we end up putting out fires instead of enjoying the outing.

Now that you are properly dressed and you are wearing a smile on your tired face you are ready to head outside and see what comes your way. Though field days are lovely and necessary, I think that a regular outing around the place where you live can teach you and your family so much about the seasons in your area and plants that grow there. You may even end up making dear friends.

We did just this when we lived on top of a mountain. We met a woman who has become a good friend, and she kept the most glorious garden. She had many native species and had resolved to have blooms in her garden for Spring, Summer and Fall. Because of our daily walks, we were able to learn the names of many plants and birds and see many that I had only learned the name of and never met in person. We even got to see some monarch caterpillars "in the wild" eating milkweed leaves. What a gift for us all!

Mother as co-learner

Now that you are outside *with* your children and you have a topic, it is time to talk about guiding and studying alongside your children. You certainly won't have all of the answers and this is good. One way to model humility is to actually be brought low enough to realize how much we truly don't know. Which is so very much. One phrase that will work on your own mind and the minds of your children is...

"I *wonder*..."

When you wonder about things out loud, it can become a bit of a game.

This is not time to get out your phone and start googling.

I know it is tempting, but for now, just wonder. Let the questions you encounter out in the *wild* work on you all during your time outside together. When you get home or have a natural break, and the question is still working on your minds, then you can see if there is an answer. Sometimes there are only theories. That is fun too.

You may wonder: "I wonder what makes some mushrooms red and some white?" or "I wonder what a wasp eats?" Or, "that flower is beautiful, I wonder what it's called?" (You can take a photo and look it up later.)

One time, we had been reading about bugs and had just learned about a spit bug. On our walk, we saw a stalk of grass at about eye level with a wad of spit resting between the stalk and the leaf blade. I was excited and said, "I wonder if there is a bug hiding inside that glob of spit!" I broke off a piece of grass and inserted it into the spittle. Sure enough, a little black bug was hiding inside. We returned him to his place, but we were now empowered with new information. We now can pass by a spit glob on a branch or grass and know that the little occupant is hiding away inside.

As a student, you will be making your own connections. You may even get excited enough to learn a few things on your own. This is great! Don't feel like you have to deliver a lecture to your scholars about all that you've learned. Some of your new knowledge will be gradually shared over time. Sometimes, you may assault your husband or friends with your new information. Great! It's fun to learn new things. Just don't get too frustrated if your scholars don't seem to care as much as you. In our home, enthusiasm catches, but it seems to have a lag-time. Perhaps it's three months? Perhaps it will be years and years. But you loving and learning about nature will if nothing else, teach them what it is to learn about and love a thing.

The Child's Role in Nature Study

Child as Observer

It's important to understand what your goals are for your scholars as you study nature together. In general, **your main objective is that they will be able to notice the world around them** with the hope that they will be able to call trees and flowers by name and have a general understanding of the way God's creation works in harmony (or cacophony) with one another.

Your goal is NOT to *make them* love nature study. It is NOT to force them to memorize lists of trees or flowers or seeds. It is not to drill the kingdoms or phylum or species of each thing they encounter. You will be leading them to nature. The leading is what you can control. They will take what they will take. What affections they develop are not up to you. Don't be discouraged if they aren't excited about what you are excited about. That's normal.

As you go out into nature and study it, remember that your chief objective for your scholars is that they would become aware of their surroundings and be able to observe nature for themselves. You may play a game if that is helpful.

Charlotte Mason, in her book *Home Education*, explains a memory game to help encourage observation and also develop oral composition skills. Lead the children into nature. Then, ask them to look around at all they see. Tell them to be careful to make a note of everything. Then, close their eyes and describe it all back to you. Take turns and see who can catch the most details and explain through all your five senses. What do you see? What do you hear? What do you smell? What do you feel? What could you taste?

Your child's role here is to simply be aware and observe. It is a delight to find that children can often remember much more than we can. They can even help us discover new things right under our noses.

Child as Co-learner

The most satisfying consequence of my decision to become more intentional with Nature Study has been seeing my children taking the reigns of their own learning. Whether it's pouring over encyclopedias or mimicking my Nature Journal entries, I can tell that they see me. But they have their own interests as well.

Sometimes a child's interest will be peaked during an outing or a reading. We can encourage or dampen this tiny spark. As you would for a friend, you will be able to learn and grow and even give your child tools to learn more.

We've found that having books about the topic we are studying prominently displayed is important. Sometimes I'll face out these books on the shelf which makes these books more likely to be picked up. Then, my readers are able to read for themselves about their areas of interest. Often, they will read to non-readers and help them also gain more knowledge apart from mother. This self-education in a non-academic area is so important that it will also spread into other subjects.

Often, we will be learning about something and need to head to the map to see where in the world it comes from. From that discovery, we may find out about a war or a historic event that happened in that region, and this may lead us to learning yet another thing. Often, our studies are not easily tucked away into neat little boxes, but they bleed over into many subjects.

A Child Set Free (with purpose)

Going outside with your children for 10-20 minutes each day can't be too much. Mothers need the sunshine and fresh air just as well as children. We also need to give our children time where they are free from our watchful eye to explore, climb, dig, etc.

In America, it is increasingly difficult to find children playing outside in neighborhoods together. Most of them are tucked safely inside their homes, glued to one blue light or another. If you are reading this, you are likely one of the few parents who crave less screen time and more time outside for your children. The first step to getting them comfortable playing outside for long stretches is for you to be outside with them. Often, what happens when you go out with your children is they see that the outside isn't so bad. In fact, it is much more exciting than the walls inside. If they are having trouble staying outside, be sure they are properly dressed and go outside with them at first. Then you can slowly wean them off of needing you. Hand them a tool such as a shovel or a rope. Both of these can provide hours of interesting play for most children.

If you use screens regularly in your home, you may need to require a certain amount of time outside prior to allowing access to a screen. I have a hard rule that on beautiful days everyone must be outside. If I need to be in the kitchen or attend to the baby, I'm usually longing to join them because great weather refreshes me to the bone.

When children are outside without you, they are able to experiment and play in a way that is different from when you are on your walk with them. They may discover a bird's nest or an ant climbing up their favorite tree. Sometimes my children will stop to watch the birds near our home and thus learn about their manners and habits. These unstructured moments are so valuable to the developing child because it allows them to not only learn about the world God created first hand, but they are developing their executive function -- they are making decisions for themselves about what they will or will not do. This is a skill that is almost non-existent in most students graduating from college. They've spent their entire childhood being told what to do and where to go so that when the real world requires that they make some decisions, many adults flounder. It's very frustrating for employers looking to hire good people.

Anyway, let them play and get dirty and don't hang over them assaulting them with stories about broken bones or broken necks. If you are that worried, set some limits, say your prayers and trust them to stay within the boundaries you've laid out. All will be well. And even when it isn't, all will be well.

In His hand are the depths of the earth, and the mountain peaks belong to Him.
The sea is His, for He made it, and His hands formed the dry land. Psalm 95:4-5

Journals

O Lord, how manifold are your works!
In wisdom have you made them all;
the earth is full of your creatures.
Here is the sea, great and wide,
which teems with creatures innumerable,
living things both small and great.
Psalm 104:24-25

One of the biggest hangups for getting my kids to use their nature journals on a regular basis was that the majority of recommendations were to bring journals out into the field and draw something while on the outing. For me, always with a very small baby and a troublesome toddler in tow, I found it torturous and frustrating to try to guide my scholars to select their specimen to draw in their nature journals. Then, to actually draw the specimen (and not a car or princess) and then color it the color God made it and not a rainbow of colors that simply never happened consistently. Why would I subject myself to this madness?

So, for a while, I stopped trying to get nature journals to happen at all.

As a listener of The Mason Jar Podcast, I heard Cindy Rollins say several times that she would simply have her children draw from nature journals while she was reading aloud. This, I could do! Sitting at a table and drawing from nature books would allow me to easily see everyone and would allow us to be a little bit more organized, plus they could hear me. Finally, they could have their colored pencils ready and not risk dropping them all over kingdom come.

This simple idea of doing nature journals inside the home sitting around the table planted a seed for me. I then started exploring how modern naturalists use their nature journals. My favorite resource is Keeping a Nature Journal by Claire Walker Leslie and Charles E. Roth. The ideas you see here combine the work and experience from this book with the work of Anna Comstock in Handbook of Nature Study and, of course, the ideas found in Charlotte Mason's writings about this topic. To get me started I decided to use Ambleside Online's Nature Study rotation selections for the current year to eliminate decision fatigue.

Now, the purpose of using the nature journal at home is to TRAIN your children how to use a field journal on their own at a later date. Laurie Bestvater encourages us in her book *The Living Page* that "the Nature Journal will have to be presented by the teacher at first… as the student gradually becomes the self-learner who relies on this companionship unconsciously." For some children this training may be a few years. For others, your structured time with nature and journaling may ignite their interest and they may start picking up their journal on their own. One of my children, within the first 12 weeks of having a plan, began picking out poetry to write into the nature journal about the current month, and later I caught that same child sketching a few different trees into the nature journal. Another child was taken by our study of the stars and planets and decided to draw an unassigned constellation into the nature journal. This shows me that we are on the right track, though my instruction will continue.

My goal is to give my children the tools they need to keep a nature journal as adults. I'm not even concerned if they decide to keep a nature journal in their adulthood or not. But, I know there will be times when they will be alone, times when they will need to focus their thoughts and ideas or even escape. If keeping a nature journal will help them, I want it to be an option. And this is why it's important that we have a plan to train the habit of using the nature journal regularly and also to teach what elements are available to be placed into a nature journal. (Hint: every subject can be utilized to study nature.)

A nature journal can be used out in the field AND can also be used inside the walls of your home. I prefer to get our kids started using a nature journal in the home at a table both *after* we've gone out and explored or perhaps even *in preparation* for an outing **to train our eyes for what to look for and help us to pay closer attention to what we see**.

"It would be well if we all persons in authority, parents and all who act for parents, could make up our minds that there is no sort of knowledge to be got in these early years so valuable to children as that which they get for themselves of the world they live in. Let them once get touch with Nature, and a habit is formed which will be a source of delight through life. We were all meant to be naturalists, each in his degree, and it is inexcusable to live in a world so full of the marvels of plant and animal life and to care for none of these things."
Home Education by Charlotte Mason pg. 61

Out-of-Doors

Never be within doors when you can rightly be without.
Charlotte Mason, *Home Education*

There are several ways in which I strive to get our children out into nature regularly. And, I confess, that even though I love to get out, even though it enriches my life, it is still a discipline to do it with regularity. What I mean is that I often don't want to go out of the house and can find a thousand excuses. The baby's schedule, my toddler has a cough, the dishes, the laundry etc all call to me as more important. And of course there is the weather. It keeps changing and once I get into a rhythm with one season, it changes and I have to adjust our patterns. I often have to coach myself to just leave the mess and get out because it is good for us all. And we all benefit by happier countenances.

The most helpful way for me to get started is to find something to go "check on" each day or each week. At one home we lived in, everyday we checked on a puddle that was in the back of a cornfield behind the property where we were living. The temperature was around 20 degrees (F) at this time, but the puddle would freeze and melt with the changing weather patterns. What we found was that the ground would also freeze into a hard rock and get slushy and muddy as the winter's rhythm progressed. Though this was not something I planned, it is a lesson that we refer back to often and even run across this type of weather and ground in the stories that we are reading. My older children have a point of reference from this experience. And these lessons that nature teaches are carried with us. All we needed to do was show up and pay attention.

At another home we lived in there were several different options, and my pattern was to take a different route each day. We checked on our neighbor's flourishing garden one day and then there was Woods Wednesday where we would check on the woods behind our home. Then on the other days, there was a route the kids could ride their bikes and yet another route where we could "check on the lake" that connected to the end of our street. There are just four days because there was usually a day for an outing with friends or our Bible Study day. I enjoyed the variety, but that is not always available.

In our current home, we only have one or two routes and they are a bit underwhelming. But still, we've seen amazing displays from the seasonal changes. One maple tree changed to a brilliant fuchsia. The biggest challenge has been our toddler. I've needed to carry, coax and discipline this child to come along with us at times. This does cut into the enjoyment of the outing, but usually when this happens I get to witness the love of siblings and find some creative ways to parent us back to the house. Usually the goal of petting the neighbor's cat does the trick. It's certainly not always "a walk in the park!"

When we have a specific topic we are studying, I will naturally draw attention to it and test myself to see if I can remember the names. Usually, I have to ask my children whose memories prove to be more faithful than mine.

It may be important to point out that **there isn't a formula that works for everyone** all the time to be able to do nature study consistently. Nature Study, instead, is a habit to cultivate -- especially for those of us for whom this way of living and paying attention to nature is new. As Charlotte Mason talks of education as an atmosphere, discipline and life we can see how these three principles play out in the context of nature study. The atmosphere is dictated by mother's attitude (and of course the attitude of the children as well, but mother leads). The discipline is the structure of a routine to get out into nature and the plan of what to study (which includes planning ahead by having the proper resources and books available to study). The life is the joy and the play, the messing in the dirt or the inspiration found in the stream or flower or even the new discovery made. This is exciting and life-giving for everyone.

I recently noticed that my mother and I have similar affections for flowers and nature. There seems to be a link and a passing along a love for nature that has happened without any real design on the part of my mother. And she shared with me that her mother and grandmother also loved pointing out beauty in nature and passed on a love of making flower arrangements. My great grandmother grew up in Germany, and in her village there was an abundance of flowers to enjoy. My mother told me this the other day:

"My mother was always pointing out beauty in nature. She always had some flowers planted. I remember in Virginia, we had a screened-in back porch and mother planted morning glories of all colors to climb up strings from the bottom to the top of the screen outside. In the summer mornings, I remember how beautiful they were and also with the dew on the spider webs in the yard. We were fortunate that we had a whole area of creek and woods behind our house that mother freely allowed us to roam—which we did!! We played Tarzan sometimes. I remember seeing the beauty of a passion flower out in the field and thinking it was the most beautiful flower I had ever seen. My sister also has the same love of flowers and making arrangements."

Isn't it wonderful that something so simple and so life-giving can bear fruit long after your life ends? May we persevere little by little, day by day. This idea is not new. Charlotte Mason affirms this same idea: *"Every human being has the power of communicating notions to other human beings; and, after he is dead, this power survives him in the work he has done and the words he has said. How illimitable is life! That the divine Spirit has like intimate power of corresponding with the human spirit, needs not to be urged, once we recognise ourselves as spiritual beings at all."* (School Education, pg. 71)

A note on group outings:
Group outings are so refreshing and helpful for mothers and children alike. With six children of various ages and stages, I've found that I can commit to one large group outing per month. I have several knowledgeable friends who have taught me how to identify different types of trees and different flowers. This helps *me* in the long run be a better guide at home or on family nature hikes.

During the month of April, our group scheduled something each week because it was peak wildflower season. This was just right. I love having a whole month dedicated to getting outside regularly with friends. What a gift!

The Tables Turned
By William Wordsworth

Up! up! my Friend, and quit your books;
Or surely you'll grow double:
Up! up! my Friend, and clear your looks;
Why all this toil and trouble?

The sun above the mountain's head,
A freshening lustre mellow
Through all the long green fields has spread,
His first sweet evening yellow.

Books! 'tis a dull and endless strife:
Come, hear the woodland linnet,
How sweet his music! on my life,
There's more of wisdom in it.

And hark! how blithe the throstle sings!
He, too, is no mean preacher:
Come forth into the light of things,
Let Nature be your teacher.

She has a world of ready wealth,
Our minds and hearts to bless—
Spontaneous wisdom breathed by health,
Truth breathed by cheerfulness.

One impulse from a vernal wood
May teach you more of man,
Of moral evil and of good,
Than all the sages can.

Sweet is the lore which Nature brings;
Our meddling intellect
Mis-shapes the beauteous forms of things:—
We murder to dissect.

Enough of Science and of Art;
Close up those barren leaves;
Come forth, and bring with you a heart
That watches and receives.

Nature Journal Prompts

Once you've picked out your topic, you will want to start using your nature journal to record your findings, start drawing or even finding poetry to describe the parts of nature you grow to love more deeply. I've included a list here of types of entries that you may include in your journals. You will notice that they aren't all of the drawing variety. As I've studied naturalists, I've found that some love to write words in their journals, some love to draw and date their art and some make lists or track measurements and statistics. In fact, there are as many ways to enter information into a nature journal as there are subjects to study. But, that's a bit overwhelming when we are starting out, isn't it? So here, I am giving you some ideas for types of entries to make in your journals. You can see it as a menu. Take what you like and leave what you don't. I've included the list on one page so that you can print it out separately to use for reference if you so desire.

At the end of this booklet, I've also included weekly lesson plans for those who would like a guide to get you started without the burden of deciding what to do next.

1. Copywork: Anatomy Page (Science/Language Arts/Art)
    a. copy parts and draw a diagram from a model
    b. parts of a flower/tree/horse/eye

2. Copywork: Theme Page (Science/Language Arts/Art)
    a. copy classification types/sizes/shapes etc (i.e. leaf shape, various angles of subject, bird feet types, tree shapes, caterpillar/chrysalis/larvae/eggs/plant it eats etc)

3. Draw Specimen: Label with common name, label with Latin name (Art, Language Arts)
    a. find an interesting fact about a subject
    b. Draw parts - i.e bud, flower, leaf, bark pattern, whole shape

4. Narration: (mother record's into Nature Journal if child is too young to write well) (Language Arts)
From a recent nature outing, record the date and location then:
    a. What did you see and where?
    b. What were the weather conditions?
    c. What did you like?
    d. What did you not like?

5. Narration: Observe a habitat - draw or write about what else lives in/on/around/under/with your subject (Science/Language Arts)

6. Rubbings, tracings and pressings (Art)

7. Phenology wheel month-by-month/day-by-day (Science)
    a. Select something with a cycle to observe
    b. Caterpillars, trees, phases of the moon, weather patterns etc

8. Phenology wheel to track one subject throughout the year (Science)

9. Find a poem about the subject and copy it into your Nature Journal (Language Arts)

10. Track growth or patterns with a bar graph (Math)

11. Learn the history of the tree you are observing, use an encyclopedia, reference book or search the Internet with you parents. Record your findings on your page.

12. Draw a map
    a. Your home, favorite hiking spot, layout of a garden, neighborhood walking route and notable plants/animals/birds you encounter

How to Use This Book

Nature Study Hacking is designed to help you guide your student through the art of studying nature and keeping a Nature Journal. These principles are old, but this application is new. The ideas from Anna Comstock's classic book *Handbook of Nature Study* are combined with the ideas of modern naturalists and educators such as Clare Walker Leslie, Charles E. Roth, Cindy Rollins and Jeannette Tulis.

The lessons are designed to be short. They begin with observation. In observing nature first-hand, we begin to develop a relationship with it that can't be duplicated. This is because we are able to engage the totality of our five senses and get to know a thing in its home. I know that when I have friends over to my home they are able to know and understand me more fully. This is the same with nature.

Reading must accompany any nature lesson. A book about nature lore or a book that describes the way these animals behave and live is essential to the study of nature. I've included the selection from Handbook of Nature Study with each animal. I've shortened them slightly and updated some of the language so that you can just jump straight to the reading while you present your lesson or perhaps you read about the animal during your Morning Time or bedtime or other family learning. (That is up to you!) Please don't skip the readings though, you will miss so much knowledge.

Diagrams are used to show or label to help teach us to call nature by name. When we know the name of something we, once again, develop a closer relationship with it. We *know* it. The lessons use copywork in order to help us remember and to know. This should be a delight and a means to the greater end of learning about nature.

With care, I've woven in a variety of types of Nature Journal entries into this series. Copywork, vocabulary, writing, math, map-making, research, reading and more are incorporated so that as you study your chosen topic, you can also explore it on a variety of levels. In addition, keeping a Nature Journal is not just about painting beautiful watercolor paintings. You will enjoy learning about many different types of entries as you go through our study together! I've designed the lessons with the aim of two lessons each week over a twelve week term. However, you can do as many or as few as you'd like. My goal is to help you establish the habit of using a Nature Journal. This book is the support to help you achieve this. It's designed to serve families first and foremost.

Lastly, throughout the study you will enjoy a few "breathing lessons." I've titled them "Review, Improve & Delight." These help us and our students to take the time and care to go back over our work and add to it, clean it up and make it better. The habit of taking the time to carefully improve our work can help us not only review what we have done, but also help us enjoy what we've done and find ways to improve it.

We'd love to hear about how you are nature study hacking! Please use #naturestudyhacking on social media if you are enjoying your booklet! Please contact us at www.naturestudyhacking.com with questions, hive fives and any ideas for improving this valuable resource for families beginning their own Nature Study Hacking journey!

Setting up Your Nature Journal

Nature Study Hacking means that there are tricks and tips to share with you to make your life simpler!

Before you begin studying and journaling you will first need to set up your journal. Be sure to use a pencil and have your eraser handy when you first start laying out your pages so that you can erase markings easily. This is YOUR journal, you are going to be working little by little to add to it just how you'd like. If you'd rather draw or paint something on a separate sheet of paper, cut it out and paste it into your notebook, you are welcome to do that. If you'd like to write directly into your notebook, that works as well! Just remember we are all learning a NEW way to use our Nature Journals, so mistakes are part of the learning process!

Here's your supply list:
1. Nature
2. [Minimalism Art sketchbook or Dot grid notebook](#) (This my favorite brand)
3. [Ticonderoga pencils and an eraser](#)
4. [Prisma colored pencils](#) (preferred for younger children)
5. Field Guide
6. Book about weather (see recommended resources)

Step 1: Now that you have your supplies, open your Nature Journal. The first page on the right of most books is called the "Title Page". This is where you will write your name, your age and "Nature Journal" - that's the Title of your book! Make sure your writing is neat and clean so that others can read it.

Step 2: Pages 1 and 2 come after the Title Page. This is called a "spread" because there are two pages "spread" together. This first page will be easiest to track and write observations you make of the one mammal you will observe over this term. Please keep this page tidy (no doodling) so that your observations can be clearly notated.

Step 3: Perpetual Journal set up: Flip to the back of your book. Starting with the last spread and working backwards (toward the front of your book), write the months of the year. I like to start with December, November etc and working my way into the center of the book until I come to January. This creates a "Perpetual Journal" where you can make entries about what you encounter during that month. You will be able to add a little bit to these pages over time. These entries can be about anything you find in nature and want to record into your Nature Journal (even if you aren't studying that topic!)

SIMPLE
LESSONS
START HERE

Introduction to Weather| Lesson 1

Reading: To begin your weather study, read 10-15 minutes from one of the following recommended books (or choose your own book to introduce weather.):
Option 1: Read aloud Chapter 1 of *Eric Sloane's Weather Book.* (Best for upper elementary and middle school.)
Option 2: Read aloud *Weather Words* by Gail Gibbons (Best for Kindergarten and lower elementary.)

Supply list:
1. Nature Journal
2. Pencil and eraser
3. Mobile device with weather app OR barometer, thermometer and wind gauge

Step 1: On the next blank page of your Nature Journal, using a ruler set up one page chart to track the weather for the next week*. For an example of the chart, see the following page.
> *Parents/Teachers may prefer to set up a sheet of paper to be on display during this week of observation as a visual reminder to check the weather. Then tape or glue into Nature Journal at the end of the week. This same chart is provided on the following page for easy copying/cutting.

Step 2: Using the tools you've selected, fill out the chart for today.

Step 3: Fill out the chart each day this week so that you begin to pay attention to how the weather feels, looks like and how the wind and barometric pressure affects your body and environment.

Note: You may use a homemade, purchased or device-based barometer, wind-tracking or temperature gauging device.
> **Younger Students:** read aloud just two pages in each sitting and then ask for an oral narration.
> **Older Students:** will be able to provide either a written or oral narration.

Weather Tracking Chart

Weather Tracking	Monday	Tuesday	Wednesday	Thursday	Friday
Wind Speed					
Temperatures High/Low					
Barometric Pressure					
Clouds/ Precipitation					

Vocabulary- Climate vs Weather| Lesson 2

Supply List:
1. Nature Journal
2. Pencil and eraser
3. Book about the Weather (see recommended resources at the end of this book)

Step 1: Read the following definitions aloud. Copy the words and definitions into your Nature Journal so that you can refer to them later.

Definitions:

Weather - the condition of the atmosphere at the moment
Climate - the sum total of weather conditions over a period of several years
Thermometer - an instrument for measuring and indicating temperature
Temperature - the degree or intensity of heat present in a substance or object
Barometer - an instrument measuring atmospheric pressure
Circulation - movement to and fro or around something
Air - the invisible gaseous substance surrounding the earth, a mixture mainly of oxygen and nitrogen
Wind - the perceptible natural movement of the air

Step 2: Compare some of these terms. What is the difference between weather and climate? What is the difference between air and wind? How are they similar? What is the difference between a thermometer and temperature?

> **Younger students:** For very young students, Parents/Teachers should just pick one word for the child to copy. The rest will be picked up as you learn more about weather.
>
> **Older students:** Write the answers to Step 2 in your Nature Journal.

Note: Please continue to read about weather from a living book so that students are seeing these terms being used properly. (See recommended resources at the end of this book.)

Source: https://dictionary.com and *Handbook of Nature Study*

Object Lesson- Evaporation| Lesson 3

Supply List:
1. Clear glass bowl
2. Plastic wrap or glass lid
3. 4 cups of hot water

Step 1: Heat water.

Step 2: Place hot water into glass bowl.

Step 3: Cover bowl with plastic wrap or glass lid. Wait and watch the steam rise and collect on the top of the lid/wrap.

Step 4: Narration questions: Which direction does the water go at first? How long before it comes back down? What must happen to the water for it to come back down? What does the water look like when it is collecting at the top? What element in nature does this remind you of? Would the same thing happen with cold water?

> **Younger students:** Draw a picture of the experiment and explain to your Parent/Teacher what you have discovered.

> **Older students:** Write a narration in your Nature Journal telling what you've discovered.

Perpetual Journal Entry| Lesson 4

Supply List:
1. Nature Journal
2. Pencil and eraser

Step 1: Go outside for five minutes and pay attention to the plants that are easy for you to see and touch.

Step 2: In your Nature Journal, in the back where you wrote the names of the months, draw a picture showing ONE thing that you observed while outside. Are the trees budding or do they have leaves? Only draw the bud or one leaf (not the whole tree). Is there a flower in bloom? Draw one flower and perhaps, the shape of the flower's leaf. Choose one thing to draw well.

Step 3: Write today's date and label your picture.

Intro to the Earth's Atmosphere| Lesson 5

Supply List:
1. Nature Journal
2. Pencil and eraser
3. *Eric Sloane's Weather Book* - Chapter 2 or watch video (see info below)

Step 1: Here are some words you will need to know about the earth's atmosphere:

Definitions:
Atmosphere - the envelope of gases surrounding the earth
Troposphere - the lowest layer of the atmosphere where all weather occurs.
Stratosphere - The layer just above the troposphere where jet airplanes fly. (This is where the ozone layer resides.)
Mesosphere - As the mesosphere extends upward above the stratosphere, temperatures decrease. The coldest parts of our atmosphere are located in this layer and can reach −90°C.
Thermosphere - In the fourth layer from Earth's surface, the thermosphere, the air is thin, meaning that there are far fewer air molecules. The thermosphere is very sensitive to solar activity and can heat up to 1,500°C or higher when the Sun is active making an aurora that lights up the night sky. Astronauts orbiting Earth in the space station or space shuttle spend their time in this layer.
Exosphere - The upper layer of our atmosphere, where atoms and molecules escape into space, is called the exosphere.

Step 2: Choose ONE to do today:
  A. Read Chapter 2 from *Eric Sloane's Weather Book*
  B. Watch video about the four spheres:
      a. **Video:** Four Spheres Part 2 (Hydro and Atmo): Crash Course Kids - https://youtu.be/UXh_7wbnS3A

Diagram of the earth's atmosphere| Lesson 6

Supply List:
1. Nature Journal
2. Pencil and eraser
3. *Eric Sloane's Weather Book* - Chapter 2 or watch video (see info below)

Step 2: Copy the diagram of the layers of the earth's atmosphere into your Nature Journal on the next blank page. (See next page.)

    Younger Students: Drawing is preferred at this age. Focus on neatness.

    Older Students: Writing and drawing can be used together. Focus on getting the details correct.

Layers of the Earth's Atmosphere

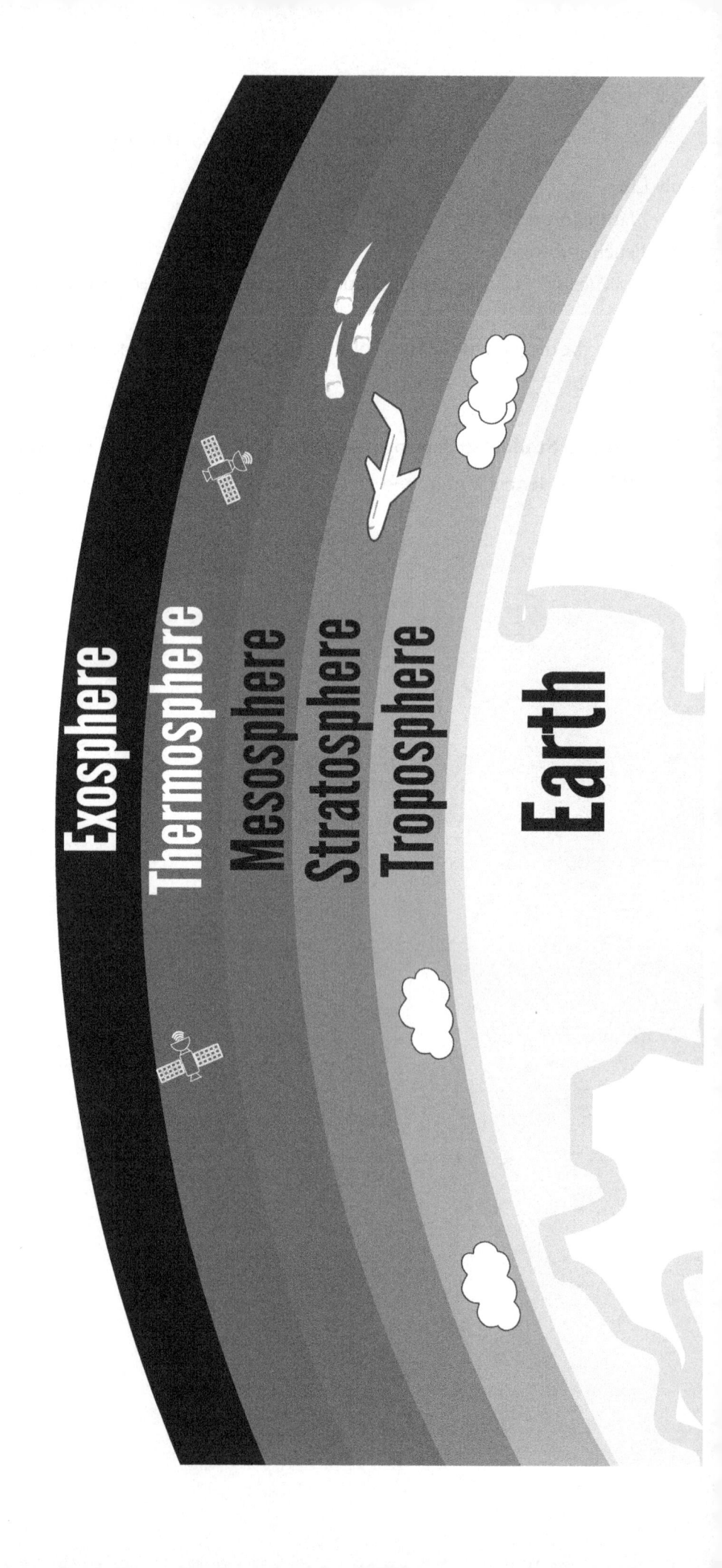

Exosphere
Thermosphere
Mesosphere
Stratosphere
Troposphere

Earth

Winds | Lesson 7

Supply List:
1. Nature Journal
2. Pencil and eraser
3. *The Lost Art of Reading Nature's Signs* **OR** *Eric Sloane's Weather Book*

Step 1: Read page 127-132 about Winds in the book *The Lost Art of Reading Nature's Signs.* **OR** Read Chapter 11 "About Winds" from *Eric Sloane's Weather Book*

Step 2: Go outside for five minutes and look for the following: where is the moon/sun in the sky? What is the wind doing? What are the clouds doing?

Step 3. Write or draw about what you learned and observed in you Nature Journal on the next blank page.

   Younger Students: Parents can write down the child's observations and narration from the reading.

   Older Students: Write your narration from the reading in your Nature Journal.

Review, Improve & Delight| Lesson 8

Supply List:
1. Nature Journal
2. Pencil and eraser
3. Pen (optional)
4. Colored pencils or watercolors
5. *Nature Study Hacking - Weather, Climate and Water* booklet

Step 1: Open your Nature Journal. Look back at the work that you have done so far. Can you add to anything you've made? Can you make anything neater? Do you need to finish your poem or add to it? Erase any extra pencil marks and trace pencil marks with ink that you like. This is your time to add color where you want and to improve the work that you've already done.

Poem| Lesson 9

Supply List:
1. Nature Journal
2. *Nature Study Hacking - Weather, Climate and Water* booklet

Step 1: Select a poem about weather that you like. In your Nature Journal, copy a verse or two from the poem. Write today's date and the name and author of the poem.

Cloud Watching| Lesson 10

Supply List:
1. Nature Journal
2. Pencil and eraser
3. Blanket or beach towel OR a window with a good view of the sky

Step 1: Go outside and find a place where you can look up and see the clouds.

Step 2: Observation questions- Are there many clouds today? Are there just a few? Where are they grouped? Do they have a pattern or shape? What color are the clouds? What color is the sky? If you wait five minutes, observe how it changes shape. Does it change quickly or slowly? What affects the speed in which the clouds change shape?

Step 3: In your Nature Journal, write today's date, the temperature, wind speed and barometric pressure. What else did you notice during your time outside. Make a note of this as well.

Younger Students: Focus on neatness. This lesson may need to be broken into a couple of days. You may substitute this for the student's copywork for this day/week.

Older Students: Focus on neatness and legibility. This lesson can be added to by using a field guide or other resource for the student to add their own insights and findings about clouds.

Clouds - Read and Watch | Lesson 11

Supply List:
1. Nature Journal
2. Pencil and eraser
3. Book about weather

Step 1: Read about the types of clouds.

Read Chapter 12 "The World of Clouds" from *Eric Sloane's Weather Book* **OR**

Read Gail Gibbons' book *Weather Words*

Step 2: Look outside and observe what types of clouds you see.

Step 3: Write or draw about what you learned from your weather book.

Younger students: Drawing is preferred

Older students: Write a couple of sentences telling what you discovered about clouds.

Cloud Types Diagram | Lesson 12

Supply List:
1. Nature Journal
2. Pencil and eraser
3. Diagram of cloud types

Step 1: Look at the diagram of cloud types on the following page.

Step 2: Set a timer for fifteen minutes. Working neatly, use this fifteen minutes to draw the types of clouds diagram into your Nature Journal. If you have time, label the cloud types as well.

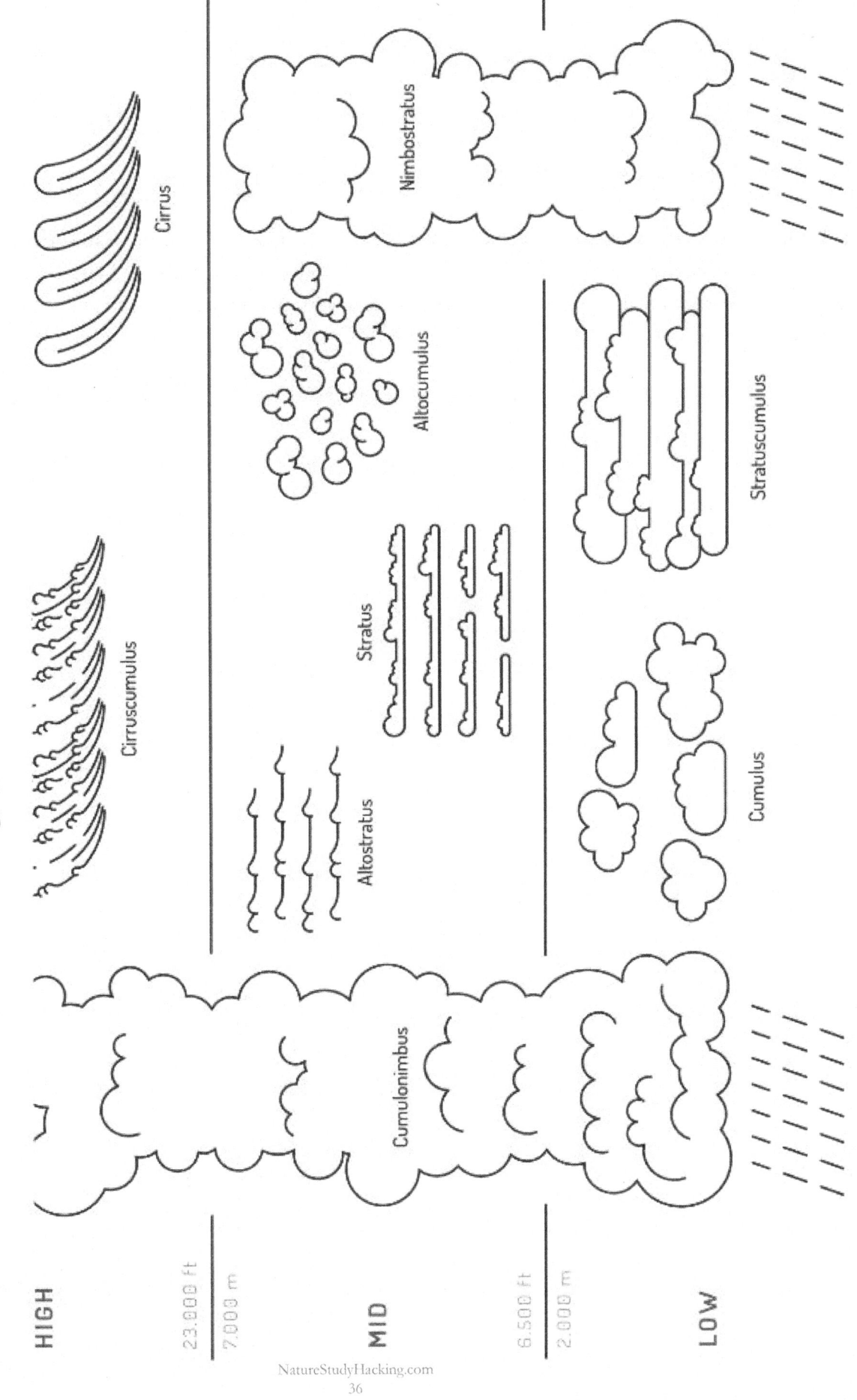

Types of Clouds

Cirrus

Cirruscumulus

Nimbostratus

Altocumulus

Altostratus

Stratus

Stratuscumulus

Cumulus

Cumulonimbus

HIGH
23,000 Ft
7,000 m

MID
6,500 Ft
2,000 m

LOW

Review, Improve & Delight| Lesson 13

Supply List:
1. Nature Journal
2. Pencil and eraser
3. Pen (optional)
4. Colored pencils or watercolors
5. *Nature Study Hacking - Weather, Climate and Water* booklet

Step 1: Open your Nature Journal. Look back at the work that you have done so far. Can you add to anything you've made? Can you make anything neater? Do you need to finish your poem or add to it? Erase any extra pencil marks and trace pencil marks with ink that you like. This is your time to add color where you want and to improve the work that you've already done.

Telling the weather| Lesson 14

Supply List:
1. Nature Journal
2. Pencil and eraser
3. Device with weather app OR thermometer, barometer and wind gauge

Step 1: Go outside and observe the weather. (Remember to start high in the sky and work your way down as you observe.) Check the temperature, the wind speed an the barometric pressure. Are there signs of precipitation?

Step 2: Make a note of these observations in your Nature Journal on the same page you wrote your poem.

>**Younger students:** May need help reading these instruments (or using a weather app). Sometimes I will copy the information into my own journal for little ones to copy more easily.

>**Older students:** Draw or write about what else they saw and other observations they made (such as plants or animals observed or cloud formations they noted during their time outside).

Telling the weather continued| Lesson 15

Supply List:
1. Nature Journal
2. Pencil and eraser
3. Device with weather app OR thermometer, barometer and wind gauge

Step 1: Go outside and observe the weather just as you did in the last lesson. (Remember to start high in the sky and work your way down as you observe.) Check the temperature, the wind speed an the barometric pressure. Is there signs of precipitation? Make a note of these in your Nature Journal on the same page you wrote your poem.

Younger Students: Focus on neatness.

Older Students: Focus on neatness and legibility. This lesson can be added to by looking up more information about observations such as wind direction, cloud formations you may see etc.

Poem| Lesson 16

Supply List:
1. Nature Journal
2. *Nature Study Hacking - Weather, Climate and Water* booklet

Step 1:. Select a poem about weather that you like. In your Nature Journal, copy a verse or two from the poem. Write today's date and the name and author of the poem.

Snow and Ice - Making Frost Demonstration | Lesson 17

Supply List:
1. Hot water
2. Clear cup
3. Timer
4. Nature Journal
5. Pencil and eraser

Step 1: Heat water to boiling.

Step 2: Take clear cup upside down and place over the steam to catch the steam. Allow it to collect until you see a bead or two of water start to drop down.

Step 3: Place cup into the freezer. Set a timer for 15 minutes.

Step 4: When the timer sounds, remove cup from the freezer.

Step 5: Answer some of the following questions: This experiment is demonstrating what happens to water when it rises into the air and cools below the freezing point. What does that do to the water? What did the water look like when it was stuck to the edges of the cup? How did it change after being in the freezer? Record your observations in your Nature Journal.

Snow and Ice Continued| Lesson 18

Supply List:
1. *The Lost Art of Reading Nature's Signs* (Chapter 17) OR *Eric Sloane's Weather Book* Chapter 12 "The World of Clouds"
2. Nature Journal
3. Pencil and eraser

Step 1: Read Chapter 17 about Snow and Sand from *The Lost Art of Reading Nature's Signs* **OR** *Eric Sloane's Weather Book* Chapter 12 "The World of Clouds"

Step 2: Write or draw a picture in your Nature Journal about what you learned in the chapter.

> **Younger Students:** Be neat and clear. You may even copy one of the diagrams from the book.

> **Older Students:** Draw a picture and write about one interesting thing about snow that you learned.

Perpetual Journal Entry| Lesson 19

Supply List:
1. Nature Journal
2. Pencil and eraser

Step 1: Go outside for five minutes and pay attention to the trees and flowers.

Step 2: In your Nature Journal, in the back where you wrote the names of the months, draw a picture showing ONE small thing that you observed while outside. Choose one thing no bigger than your fist to draw well.

Step 3: Write today's date and label your picture.

Rain and Lightning| Lesson 20

Supply List:
1. Nature Journal
2. Pencil and eraser
3. *Eric Sloane's Weather Book*

Step 1: Read from *Eric Sloane's Weather Book* pages 71-77

Step 2: Choose one of the diagrams from the reading to copy into your Nature Journal.

> **Younger Students:** Focus on neatness. This lesson may take two or three sittings to complete. Limit to 15 minutes or have student copy diagram while you read aloud the selection.

> **Older Students:** Writing and drawing can be used together. Focus on getting the details correct. This lesson may take two or three sittings to complete.

Rain and Lightning Continued| Lesson 21

Supply List:
1. Nature Journal
2. Pencil and eraser
3. *Eric Sloane's Weather Book*

Step 1: Continue working on your Nature Journal entry from the reading and diagram copying from the last lesson.

Step 2: Consider these questions: How does the water get into the cloud? What makes lightning? What does it make a sound? Why does it make light? Is there anything in your home that is similar to this reaction? What makes the rain in the cloud come back to the ground?

Rainbow Experiment| Lesson 22

Supply List:
1. Glass of water
2. Morning or Evening Sunlight is best
3. White paper
4. Nature Journal
5. Pencil and eraser

Step 1: Find a place with full sunlight.

Step 2: Place the glass of water in the sunlight. Then place a piece of white paper under the glass of water so that the sun is behind the glass of water. The sun needs to shine through the glass of water and onto a sheet of paper. Then you will see a rainbow or prism.

Step 3: Record your findings in your Nature Journal. Why does the rainbow appear? Will it still appear through the glass without water? Why or why not?

Draw a Rainbow | Lesson 23

Supply List:
1. Nature Journal
2. Pencil and eraser

Step 1: On your next blank page of your Nature Journal, draw a rainbow in your nature journal. Be sure to keep the colors in their proper order:

red, orange, yellow, green, blue, indigo and violet.

Perpetual Journal Entry| Lesson 24

Supply List:
1. Nature Journal
2. Pencil and eraser
3. Book of Poetry or *Nature Study Hacking* book

Step 1: Go outside for five minutes and pay attention to the weather, sights and sounds.

Step 2: In your Nature Journal, in the back you wrote the names of the months. Under the current month, draw or write about today's weather. What are the sounds you hear? What do you see when you look up? What do you see down? Sit quietly and pay attention. What does the weather feel like? Do you like it? If it's too hot or cold to be outside for too long, step outside and feel how the temperature hits your skin.

Weather| Exam Week

Supply List:
1. Nature Journal
2. Pencils and eraser

Step 1: Look through your Nature Journal you created this term. Look at the pages where you recorded information about the weather, clouds, wind and water. Spend about 5-10 minutes.

Step 2: Tell your parent all you know about the weather. You may use your Nature Journal to demonstrate and show examples of what you remember. Be sure to include the most interesting thing that you learned.

(Note to parent: you may choose to write down what your child says or record their narration on video.)

Poems about Weather

A Calendar
by Sara Coleridge

January brings the snow,
Makes our feet and fingers glow.

February brings the rain,
Thaws the frozen lake again.

March brings breezes, loud and shrill,
To stir the dancing daffodil.

April brings the primrose sweet,
Scatters daisies at our feet.

May brings flocks of pretty lambs
Skipping by their fleecy dams.

June brings tulips, lilies, roses,
Fills the children's hands with posies.

Hot July brings cooling showers,
Apricots and gillyflowers.

August brings the sheaves of corn,
Then the harvest home is borne.

Warm Septemper brings the fruit;
Sportsmen then begin to shoot.

Fresh October brings the pheasant;
Then to gather nuts is pleasant.

Dull November brings the blast;
Then the leaves are whirling fast.

Chill December brings the sleet,
Blazing fire, and Christmas treat.

O wind, why do you never rest
by Christina Rossetti

O wind, why do you never rest
Wandering, whistling to and fro,
Bringing rain out of the west,
From the dim north bringing snow?

There's snow on the fields
by Christina Rossetti

There's snow on the fields,
And cold in the cottage,
While I sit in the chimney nook
Supping hot pottage.

My clothes are soft and warm,
Fold upon fold,
But I'm so sorry for the poor
Out in the cold.

I dug and dug amongst the snow
by Christina Rossetti

I dug and dug amongst the snow,
And thought the flowers would never grow;
I dug and dug amongst the sand,
And still no green thing came to hand.

Melt, O snow! the warm winds blow
To thaw the flowers and melt the snow;
But all the winds from every land
Will rear no blossom from the sand.

Fog
by Carl Sandburg

The fog comes
on little cat feet.

It sits looking
over harbor and city
on silent haunches
and then moves on.

Rain
by Robert Louis Stevenson

The rain is raining all around,
    It falls on field and tree,
It rains on the umbrellas here,
    And on the ships at sea.

Raining
by Amelia Josephine Burr

Raining, raining,
All night long;
Sometimes loud, sometimes soft,
Just like a song.

There'll be rivers in the gutters
And lakes along the street.
It will make our lazy kitty
Wash his little dirty feet.

The roses will wear diamonds
Like kings and queens at court;
But the pansies all get muddy
Because they are so short.

I'll sail my boat to-morrow
In wonderful new places,
But first I'll take my watering-pot
And wash the pansies' faces.

Weather
Author unknown

Whether the weather be fine
Or whether the weather be not,
Whether the weather be cold
Or whether the weather be hot,
We'll weather the weather
Whatever the weather,
Whether we like it or not.

Before the Rain
by Thomas Bailey Aldrich

We knew it would rain, for all the morn
    A spirit on slender ropes of mist
Was lowering its golden buckets down
    Into the vapory amethyst.

Of marshes and swamps and dismal fens--
    Scooping the dew that lay in the flowers,
Dipping the jewels out of the sea,
    To sprinkle them over the land in showers.

We knew it would rain, for the poplars showed
    The white of their leaves, the amber grain
Shrunk in the wind--and the lightning now
    Is tangled in tremulous skeins of rain!

After the Rain
by Thomas Bailey Aldrich

The rain has ceased, and in my room
    The sunshine pours an airy flood;
And on the church's dizzy vane
    The ancient cross is bathed in blood.

From out the dripping ivy leaves,
    Antiquely carven, gray and high,
A dormer, facing westward, looks
    Upon the village like an eye.

And now it glimmers in the sun,
    A globe of gold, a disk, a speck;
And in the belfry sits a dove
    With purple ripples on her neck.

The Wind in a Frolic
by William Howitt

The wind one morning sprang up from sleep,
Saying, "Now for a frolic! now for a leap!
Now for a madcap galloping chase!
I'll make a commotion in every place!"
So it swept with a bustle right through a great town,
Cracking the signs and scattering down
Shutters; and whisking, with merciless squalls,
Old women's bonnets and gingerbread stalls.
There never was heard a lustier shout,
As the apples and oranges trundled about;
And the urchins that stand with their thievish eyes
Forever on watch, ran off each with a prize.

Then away to the field it went, blustering and humming,
And the cattle all wondered whatever was coming;
And tossed the colts' manes all over their brows;
It plucked by the tails the grave matronly cows,
Till, offended at such an unusual salute,
They all turned their backs, and stood sulky and mute.

So on it went capering and playing its pranks,
Whistling with reeds on the broad river's banks,
Puffing the birds as they sat on the spray,
Or the traveler grave on the king's highway.
It was not too nice to hustle the bags
Of the beggar, and flutter his dirty rags;
'Twas so bold that it feared not to play its joke
With the doctor's wig or the gentleman's cloak.

Through the forest it roared, and cried gaily, "Now,
You sturdy old oaks, I'll make you bow!"
And it made them bow without more ado,
Or it cracked their great branches through and through.

Then it rushed like a monster on cottage and farm,
Striking their dwellers with sudden alarm;
And they ran out like bees in a midsummer swarm;--
There were dames with their kerchiefs tied over their caps,
To see if their poultry were free from mishaps;
The turkeys they gobbled, the geese screamed aloud,
And the hens crept to roost in a terrified crowd;
There was rearing of ladders, and logs laying on,
Where the thatch from the roof threatened soon to be gone.

But the wind had swept on, and had met in a lane
With a schoolboy, who panted and struggled in vain;
For it tossed him and twirled him, then passed, and he stood
With his hat in a pool and his shoes in the mud.
There was a poor man, hoary and old,
Cutting the heath in the open wold;
The strokes of his bill were faint and few
Ere this frolicsome wind upon him blew,
But behind him, before him, about him it came,
And the breath seemed gone from his feeble frame;
So he sat him down, with a muttering tone,
Saying, "Plague on the wind! was the like ever known?
But nowadays every wind that blows
Tells me how weak an old man grows."

But away went the wind in its holiday glee,
And now it was far on the billowy sea,
And the lordly ship felt its staggering blow,
And the little boats darted to and fro.
But lo! it was night, and it sank to rest
On the sea-bird's rock in the gleaming west,
Laughing to think, in its fearful fun,
How little of mischief it really had done.

Who Has Seen the Wind?
by Christina Rossetti

Who has seen the wind?
    Neither I nor you:
But when the leaves hang trembling,
    The wind is passing through.

Who has seen the wind?
    Neither you nor I:
But when the trees bow down their heads,
    The wind is passing by.

The Rainbow
by Christina Rossetti

Boats sail on the rivers,
    And ships sail on the seas;
But clouds that sail across the sky
    Are prettier than these.

There are bridges on the rivers,
    As pretty as you please;
But the bow that bridges heaven,
    And overtops the trees,
And builds a road from earth to sky,
    Is prettier far than these.

Little Raindrops
by Jane Euphemia Browne

Oh, where do you come from,
    You little drops of rain,
Pitter patter, pitter patter,
    Down the window pane?

They won't let me walk,
    And they won't let me play,
And they won't let me go
    Out of doors at all today.

They put away my playthings
    Because I broke them all,
And then they locked up all my bricks,
    And took away my ball.

Tell me, little raindrops,
    Is that the way you play,
Pitter patter, pitter patter,
    All the rainy day?

They say I'm very naughty,
    But I've nothing else to do
But sit here at the window;
    I should like to play with you.

The little raindrops cannot speak,
    But "pitter pitter pat"
Means, "We can play on this side,
    Why can't you play on that?"

Resources

Books about Weather:
Eric Sloane's Weather Book by Eric Sloane (Living book explaining the weather.)
Look at the Sky... and tell the weather by Eric Sloane (Stories about people interacting with the weather in various ways. Excellent as a read aloud for Morning Time or assigned reading for an older student.)
The Lost Art of Reading Nature Signs by Tristan Gooley (Explanations of how to read weather, clouds and winds.)
Weather Words by Gail Gibbons (This book is a great introduction to weather for elementary age children.)
Weather Forecasting by Gail Gibbons (This book is an introduction to the tools used to predict and track the weather.)
Nature Anatomy and *Farm Anatomy* by Julia Rotham (Excellent for copying drawings into Nature Journal.)

Handbook of Nature Study:
Weather and Climate, p. 780-807
Water, p. 808-814

Nature Study Essentials:
Handbook of Nature Study by Anna Comstock
Nature Anatomy by Julia Rothman

Nature Lore Book List:
http://sabbathmoodhomeschool.com/charlotte-mason-living-science/nature-lore-books/

Nature Drawing help for early elementary:
How to Draw Almost Everything by Chika Miyata

PNEU Articles on Nature Study as inspiration:
https://www.amblesideonline.org/PR/PR07p332NaturalHistory.shtml
https://www.amblesideonline.org/PR/PR41p000CharmNatureStudy.shtml

YouTube Playlist:
https://www.youtube.com/user/joycherrick/playlists

Supply List:
1. Blank Journal - Minimalism Art sketchbook or Dot grid notebook (This my favorite brand)
2. Ticonderoga pencils and an eraser
3. Prisma colored pencils (preferred for younger children)
4. Field Guide
5. Books about the Weather (see list above)

Books in the
Nature Study Hacking Series

Nature Study Hacking - Trees

Nature Study Hacking - Stars & Skies

Nature Study Hacking - Mammals

Nature Study Hacking - Weather

Nature Study Hacking - Cultivated Crops and Weeds

Get updates about when we release new books by signing up at
NatureStudyHacking.com

#naturestudyhacking

Terms of Use:
Copyright Joy Cherrick All right reserved.
You may not create anything to sell or share based on this product.
This product is for one teacher use only.
All poems used herein are in the public domain.
Designed and formatted by Joy Cherrick.

(The downloadable version of this document contains affiliate links)

Made in United States
Orlando, FL
11 February 2024

Made in the USA
Monee, IL
22 December 2020

About the Author

Mrs. Leane VanderPutten lives in rural Kansas with her husband of over 30 years. She is the mother and grandmother of 11 children and 23 grandchildren, and growing.....

They are devoted to Tradition within the Fold of the Catholic Church, homeschoolers, with 5 children still at home.

Their family life is lively...full of faith and joy!

At the End of Your Day....

HITHERTO... HENCEFORTH

Hitherto the Lord hath helped us,
Guiding all the way;
Henceforth let us trust Him fully,
Trust Him all the day.

Hitherto the Lord hath loved us,
Caring for His own;
Henceforth let us love Him better,
Live for Him alone.

Hitherto the Lord hath blessed us,
Crowning all our days;
Henceforth let us live to bless Him,
Live to show His praise.

As to the examination of conscience, which we all should make before going to bed, you know the rules:

Thank God for having preserved you through the day past.

Examine how you have conducted yourself through the day, in order to which recall where and with whom you have been, and what you have done. If you have done anything good, offer thanks to God; if you have done amiss in thought, word, or deed, ask forgiveness of His Divine Majesty, resolving to confess the fault when opportunity offers, and to be diligent in doing better.

Then commend your body and soul, the Church, your relations and friends, to God. Ask that the Saints and Angels may keep watch over you, and with God's Blessing go to the rest He has appointed for you.

Neither this practice nor that of the morning should ever be omitted; by your morning prayer you open your soul's windows to the sunshine of righteousness, and by your evening devotions you close them against the shades of hell.

-St. Francis de Sales

Good Night To Our Blessed Mother

Night is falling dear Mother, the long day is o'er!
And before thy loved image I am kneeling once more,
To thank thee for keeping me safe through the day;
To ask thee this night to keep evil away.
Many times have I fallen today, Mother Dear,
Many graces neglected, since last I knelt here;
Wilt thou not in pity, my own Mother mild,
Ask Jesus to pardon the sins of thy child?
I am going to rest, for the day's work is done,
Its hours and its moments have passed one by one;
And the God who will judge me has noted them all,
He has numbered each grace, He has counted each fall.
In His book they are written against the last day,
O Mother, ask Jesus to wash them away;
For one drop of His blood which for sinners was spilt,
Is sufficient to cleanse the whole world of its guilt.
And if ere the dawn I should draw my last breath,
And the sleep that I take be the long sleep of death,
Be near me, dear Mother, for dear Jesus' sake
When my soul on Eternity's shore shall awake.

Goodnight, my Guardian Angel, dear!
I thank thee, spirit bright.
For thy sweet love and constant care,
Thy guidance and thy light.
From sin and harm preserve me still,
Nor let vain fears affright;
Conform my heart to God's dear will,
Sweet Angel mine, good night!

Visit, we beseech Thee, O Lord, this habitation, and drive far from it all snares of the enemy; let Thy holy Angels dwell herein, to preserve us in peace; and let Thy blessing be upon us forever. Through Christ our Lord. Amen.

Where Are You Going?
-Rev. George A. Kelly, 1950's

Before you can make any real decisions about the kind of adult you want to be and the kind of life you want to lead, you obviously must understand why you were born in the first place.

If you don't know, you'd be like a man who awoke one morning and found himself on a strange planet about which he knew nothing. He might be amused or interested by this sight or that, but he'd miss the entire meaning of what he saw and he'd be unable to find any significance in his entire journey.

Fortunately, you can know why you're here. You are here because God put you here. As God's handiwork you reflect Him, His planning, and His Glory. You are expected to pay homage to your heavenly Father and to use your talents well.

This is no lasting city, you know, for even the young have seen death. But if you complete your earthly mission successfully, you will be given a home with God forever.

Therefore, as you look to your future, keep this goal always before you. What does it profit you if you attain worldly success, wealth, or pleasure, and at the end of your life find to your dismay that you have not lived as God wanted you to?

The eternal displeasure of God is a terrifying thought for anyone tempted to forget that God has definite ideas of how you shall spend your life.

Soon you'll have to answer hundreds of other questions concerning your life – questions about your future, your vocation, the conduct of your business affairs, about marriage and parenthood.

If you're like the rest of us, you won't know the best answers at once. But if you make sure that your answers to all these little questions will match the right answer to the big question – if you constantly ask whether this act you're considering, this goal you're seeking, will help you save your soul – you'll have a standard to guide you. No matter what's happening around you, you'll be secure; you'll have something sturdy and unyielding to cling to.

You can find your security in the teaching of the Church. She has the answer to any and all specific problems regarding your relationship with Almighty God.

You needn't – in fact, you must not – depend entirely upon yourself to make sure that you're serving God in this world in the way He wants. By following the teaching of the Church, however, you can always know that you're on the right path.

Siblings

Friendships in the family require care and culture—as do other friendships. We must win one another's love inside the home doors just as we win the love of outside friends. We must prove ourselves worthy; we must show ourselves unselfish, self forgetful, thoughtful, and kind, tender, patient, helpful. Then when we have won each other we must keep the treasure of affection and confidence, just as we do in the case of friends not in the sacred circle of home.
-J.R. Miller

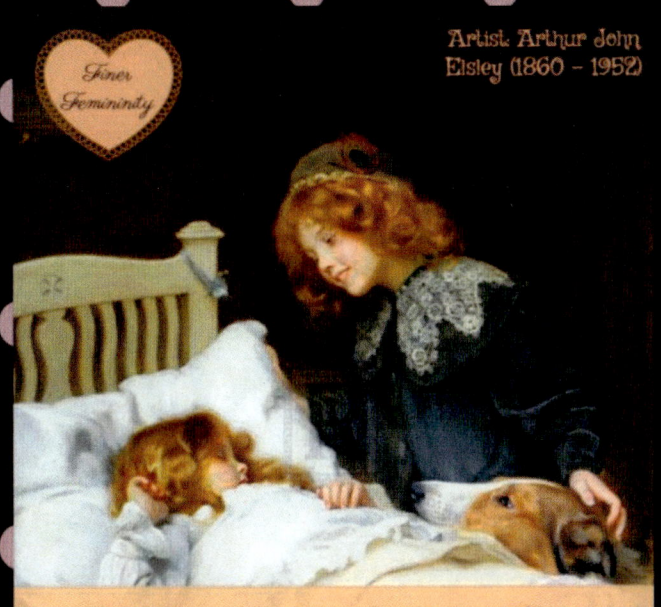

Artist: Arthur John Elsley (1860 – 1952)

Brothers and sisters are each other's natural keepers. If they fulfilled their duties in this regard, the one to the other, life would show fewer wrecks. They should shield each other. They should be an inspiration to each other in the direction of all noble thought and better life. They should be each other's guardian angels in this world of danger and of false and fatal paths. -J.R. Miller

A full and complete family, is one in which brothers and sisters all dwell together in tender love. We all know such homes, where the family life is full—and the family fellowship close, caring and happy; where parents and children, and brothers and sisters—live together in sweet accord, and where the music of the daily life is like an unbroken song of holy peace. Wherever there is such a home, its blessedness is almost heavenly!
-J.R. Miller

Religious Life
(Continued)

Who hasn't heard someone mention after a trip to the convent how happy the nuns all seemed! Their faces shone with joy! I've heard this more than once about the cloistered nuns in the Carmel in Nebraska! And these sisters are more secluded than the other orders! Does this make them somber and melancholic?? It doesn't seem so! God has given them much more than they have given Him. He is not outdone! If, to a woman, whose very existence is said to love, there is offered an ideal worth all she has to give for it, this is it. As long as she is loyal, Jesus will never disappoint her, but He will always surpass her most ardent expectations and her most glowing prospect of the holiest and sweetest friendships and love.

On earth, in the midst of all the privations of convent life, He will give her the peace that the world does not know and cannot give and which exceeds all the happiness the world gives. And this is nothing compared to what He has prepared for them in heaven!

When Our Lord whispers His invitation and she answers this call unselfishly and wholeheartedly, her example will often draw many others and start a long procession of girls joyously making for the house of the Lord.

She will be given credit for these virgins following her lead.

And, though the religious life has its hardships, to those whom God calls, He will make their life not only bearable, but even welcome, sweet, enjoyable and thoroughly and intensely delicious. Happy are those whom He has chosen!

I always find a way of being happy...
~St. Therese of Lisieux

www.saintbenedict.com • facebook.com/SistersMICM

The Religious Life
Based on writings of Fr. Fulgence Meyer, 1927

There are three kinds of vocations that come into consideration. A young lady may be called by God either to lead a single life in the world, or to consecrate herself to God in the religious life or to be married. One of these three roles is fixed by God for everyone, and it is in the best interest of the young person to find out his calling early in life, in order to prepare for and to be better qualified for it when the time comes.

The Church has declared that the religious life, when embraced and followed from motives, is in itself holier and more acceptable before God than life in marriage, since it involves greater sacrifice of oneself.

This does not mean that just because one has chosen a higher state, that she is more virtuous than someone in a lower state.

It happens frequently that a married person has more virtue than one in a religious state, because they live up to their duties more perfectly. If one is married and tries to do her duty cheerfully, changing the diapers, serving her husband when it is hard, staying up nights with the children without complaining, this woman will have more virtue than the religious who complains about her aches and pains, or her other fellow nuns who annoy her.

This being said, it still remains that the religious state is dearer to God than the married state.

A large number of young ladies are called to the religious life. This is vocation in its highest degree. This being the highest of calls, Our Lord spoke solemnly, "You have not chosen Me: but I have chosen you; and have appointed you, that you should go and should bring forth fruit, and your fruit should remain." The words of Our Lord come to mind, "Many are called, but few are chosen."

A king may love and smile upon the multitude of his subjects and favor them variously; but only a few chosen ones he invites into the inner apartments of his palace to make them his intimates and confidantes.

Jesus asks these special chosen to tenderly be his own dear and consecrated spouses.

My husband tells our girls that if they are looking for THE perfect man of their dreams, look no further! If they want to marry their ideal, go for the religious life and make Jesus their spouse. He won't let them down!

If young girls devote their youth, health, talents, energies and all their sufferings and sacrifices exclusively to Him, He will, in turn, protect and comfort them in His loving arms and they will enjoy a happiness unsurpassed! (Continued on next page.)

Quotes

"Few things have so powerful a determining effect upon a person's subsequent life as the taste for and the habit of reading acquired in youth. Hence the necessity of conceiving a love for good reading, and of nursing the practice of it in the earliest years. Catholic young people are very fortunate, if they relish the reading of not only good, but of the best books, papers and magazines within their reach."
Rev. Fulgence Meyer, 1927

"The thought is very beautiful—that youth must gather the sweet things of life—the flowers, the fragrant odors, which lie everywhere, so that old age may be clothed with gladness. We do not realize how much of the happiness of our after years, will depend upon the things we are doing today. It is our own life that gives color to our skies, and tone to the music that we hear in this world. The song or the discord which rings in our ears—we may think it is made by other voices—but it is really the echo of our own yesterdays."
- J.R. Miller

"Ask a great deal of the boy; but bring the boy a great deal yourself. It's a shabby marriage when either party short-changes the other in disposition, virtue, devotion and faith." -Rev. Daniel A. Lord

"The Rosary is a powerful weapon to put the demons to flight and to keep oneself from sin…If you desire peace in your hearts, in your homes, and in your country, assemble each evening to recite the Rosary. Let not even one day pass without saying it, no matter how burdened you may be with many cares and labors."
– Pope Pius XI

"But you are a great fool indeed if you allow yourself to fall in love with someone not of your faith. The plain fact is that nothing so disqualifies a man for marriage to you as the lack of your religious faith or the acceptance of a religion that regards your religion as false, misleading, and perhaps even of the devil. Marry the man of your own faith."
-Rev. Daniel A. Lord, 1950's

Quotes

"What is our conversation like each day, especially with the members of our family? Do we continually talk about depressing news, do we regularly voice our negative opinions about the people and situations around us? Do we talk about our own sufferings and our needs in a complaining manner? How about a different approach? Let's talk about the positive instead. If we are talking of people, let's make the effort to only bring up the good. Want to talk about heroes? Our grandparents, parents, ordinary folk and how they have overcome obstacles would be a good testimony to your kids. We all have stories to tell….make sure they are bringing out the best in those who are listening!"
– Finer Femininity

"If you're like the rest of us, you won't know the best answers to life at once. But if you make sure that your answers to all the little questions will match the right answer to the big question – if you constantly ask whether this act you're considering, this goal you're seeking, will help you save your soul – you'll have a standard to guide you. No matter what's happening around you, you'll be secure; you'll have something sturdy and unyielding to cling to."
–The Catholic Youth's Guide to Life and Love, Rev. George A. Kelly

"Like a knife, the tongue has a sharp, powerful edge that can either be used to heal or destroy. A knife in the hands of a skilled surgeon brings healing and life, but a knife in the hands of a felon brings death and destruction. Like the surgeon, we can study how to use our mouths to bring life to those around us. But it's not easy, and the tongue is difficult to control."
– Sharon Jaynes, The Power of a Woman's Words

"True beauty comes from within. If that beauty is lacking, no exercise program, eating plan, or wardrobe update can put it there. No interior decorating scheme can give it to me. "The unfading beauty of a gentle and quiet spirit... is of great worth in God's sight." 1 Peter 3:4
– Emilie Barnes.

(Continued) What Friendship Ought to Be

Beware of intimacies with a member of the opposite sex, for such a friendship is nearly always dangerous; still less ought you to entertain friendships which are unworthy of the name.

I refer to sinful connections, or keeping company, that are the occasion of sin. This subject I shall treat at greater length in another place.

In the mean time I will make only one remark, namely this, that until you are at least eighteen years of age you should not keep regular company or cultivate familiar friendship with a person of the opposite sex.

I wish most earnestly to impress upon you the necessity for watchfulness and prayer in order that your understanding may not be perverted by the indulgence of your senses and your passions.

Do not say, as so many do, that the heart, the power of love, cannot be restrained. How greatly were you to be pitied if you were so weak of character as to surrender yourself to the sway of sensual affection!

Be not hasty in forming close friendships. "But when you have found a friend," says a certain writer, "let neither life nor death, nor misunderstanding, nor distance, nor doubt, nor anything else interrupt this friendship and vex your peace."

You must exercise self-control in friendship. Be patient, be kind, be thoughtful, unselfish and loyal under all circumstances. Be true to your friends. Let their joys be your joys, and their sorrows your sorrows.

A friend is one of the sweetest things that life can bring. A true friend is not only our comfort in sorrow, our help in adversity; he also recalls us to a sense of duty, when we have forgotten ourselves, he inspires and encourages us to aim at high ideals, he takes loving heed of our health, our work, our plans and all that concerns us; he wants to make us good and happy.

Sweeter than the breath of spring,
Is the joy a friend can bring,
Who rejoices in our gladness
And gives solace in our sadness.

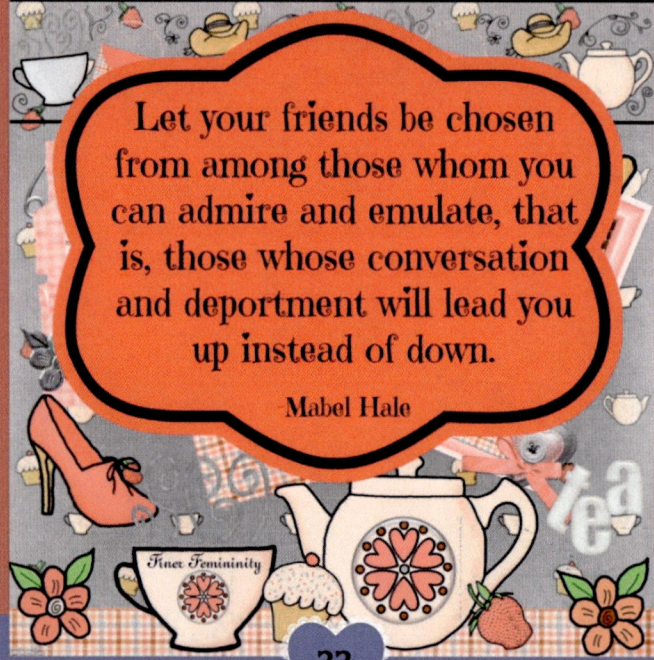

> Let your friends be chosen from among those whom you can admire and emulate, that is, those whose conversation and deportment will lead you up instead of down.
>
> — Mabel Hale

What Friendship Ought to Be
Fr. F.X. Lasance, 1905

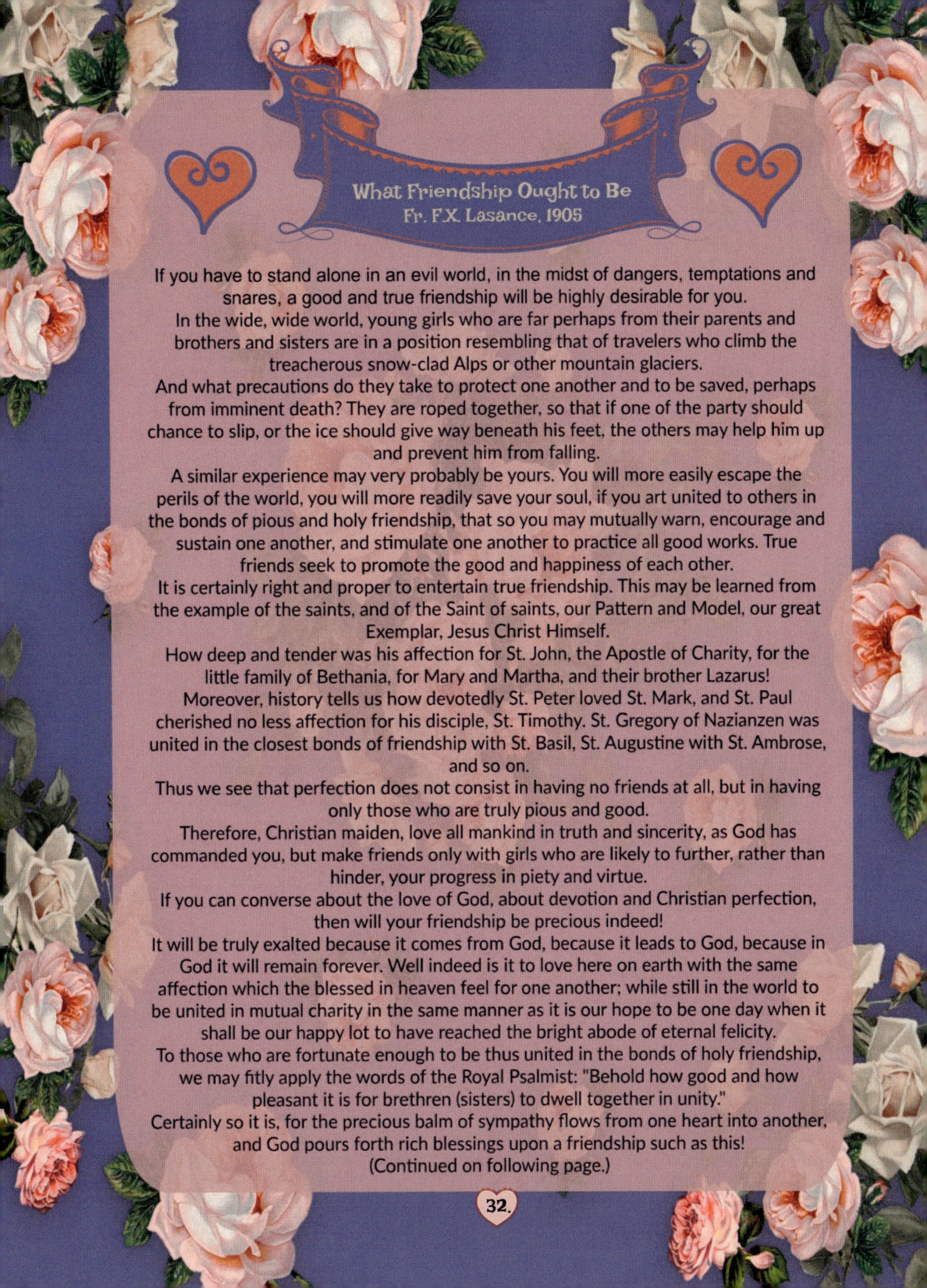

If you have to stand alone in an evil world, in the midst of dangers, temptations and snares, a good and true friendship will be highly desirable for you.

In the wide, wide world, young girls who are far perhaps from their parents and brothers and sisters are in a position resembling that of travelers who climb the treacherous snow-clad Alps or other mountain glaciers.

And what precautions do they take to protect one another and to be saved, perhaps from imminent death? They are roped together, so that if one of the party should chance to slip, or the ice should give way beneath his feet, the others may help him up and prevent him from falling.

A similar experience may very probably be yours. You will more easily escape the perils of the world, you will more readily save your soul, if you art united to others in the bonds of pious and holy friendship, that so you may mutually warn, encourage and sustain one another, and stimulate one another to practice all good works. True friends seek to promote the good and happiness of each other.

It is certainly right and proper to entertain true friendship. This may be learned from the example of the saints, and of the Saint of saints, our Pattern and Model, our great Exemplar, Jesus Christ Himself.

How deep and tender was his affection for St. John, the Apostle of Charity, for the little family of Bethania, for Mary and Martha, and their brother Lazarus!

Moreover, history tells us how devotedly St. Peter loved St. Mark, and St. Paul cherished no less affection for his disciple, St. Timothy. St. Gregory of Nazianzen was united in the closest bonds of friendship with St. Basil, St. Augustine with St. Ambrose, and so on.

Thus we see that perfection does not consist in having no friends at all, but in having only those who are truly pious and good.

Therefore, Christian maiden, love all mankind in truth and sincerity, as God has commanded you, but make friends only with girls who are likely to further, rather than hinder, your progress in piety and virtue.

If you can converse about the love of God, about devotion and Christian perfection, then will your friendship be precious indeed!

It will be truly exalted because it comes from God, because it leads to God, because in God it will remain forever. Well indeed is it to love here on earth with the same affection which the blessed in heaven feel for one another; while still in the world to be united in mutual charity in the same manner as it is our hope to be one day when it shall be our happy lot to have reached the bright abode of eternal felicity.

To those who are fortunate enough to be thus united in the bonds of holy friendship, we may fitly apply the words of the Royal Psalmist: "Behold how good and how pleasant it is for brethren (sisters) to dwell together in unity."

Certainly so it is, for the precious balm of sympathy flows from one heart into another, and God pours forth rich blessings upon a friendship such as this!

(Continued on following page.)

Duties Towards Parents
(con't)

Another question is, why is the fourth the only one of the Ten Commandments for the observance of which is promised also an earthly reward? Again because of its supreme importance, and to stimulate its due fulfilment. Then, too, its very keeping involves and produces terrestrial happiness. The consciousness of being right with father and mother, and of paying them the tribute of love and reverence that is their due, is in itself one of the sweetest feelings the human breast experiences. Besides, the good feelings begotten by the sweet relations of attachment and good-will between parents and children make for mental and corporal comfort and happiness in the home and elsewhere, and thereby strongly act in favor of a blissful longevity.

The Secret of Life's Success

The qualities that concur in disposing a child to honor, obey and love its parents, are good sense, self-control, self-discipline, regularity, system, order, moderation and disinterested devotion to duty. These are the same traits that spell success and happiness in life in general. In addition to God's special blessing they bring about the fulfilment of the words of the Bible: "He that honoreth his mother is as one that layeth up a treasure. He that honoreth his father shall have joy in his own children" (Ecclus.,3,5,6). This last remark is noteworthy. It tells that the reward of good children will be after the manner of their virtue. For being good and loving to their parents, their own children, once they themselves are parents, will be good and loving to them. To obtain this boon, no sacrifice is too great.

"You are a young lady and obedience is very important to learn now. When you become a young woman and choose a vocation, whether it be the religious life or a wife and mother, obedience is a very important virtue for both of these vocations. The more you learn to be obedient now, the easier it will be later in life and the sweeter your life will be.

St. Francis de Sales says that he who is obedient will live sweetly and will be like a child in the arms of his mother, free from worry and from care. That's a pretty awesome promise!

Even if you see faults in your parents (and you will see them because they are only human) you need to always show respect.

The Fourth Commandment does not say to honor a good or a perfect mother and father, it says to honor your mother and father. Period." -Finer Femininity

Duties Towards Parents

by Fr. Fulgence Meyer, Youth's Pathfinder, 1927

"He that honoreth his mother is as one that layeth up a treasure. He that honoreth his father shall enjoy a long life" (Ecclus., 3, 5, 7)

After God no one has done or does so much for a child as its parents. To them it owes the greatest boon it has: the gift of existence. It does not require much reflection to become aware that existence is the root and spring of every good we possess. Friendship, love, happiness, success and fame cannot even be conceived without it. We are glad and thankful for many things. The one thing we must rejoice over and thank for most is the fact of our existence. And since God used our parents to confer upon us this priceless gift, and since without this particular man and woman, who are our parents, we should never have existed at all, there is nothing more natural than that for this favor alone, and were it the only one we received from them, we entertain for them the liveliest feeling of love, respect and gratitude as long as we live.

The Inerasable Claim to Honor

No matter what else parents may or may not be or do to their child, and however recreant they may be to their parental duties, and personally unworthy of respect and honor: the mere fact, that they were the agents God employed to give existence to the child, so that without these particular parents the child would have never been, must outweigh far and away every consideration of a personal nature that is unfavorable to them, or threatens to militate against the love, reverence and recognition their dignity as parents demands..

Why the Distinction?

The first question that rises in our minds in connection with this command is: Why does God in the Ten Commandments inculcate so solemnly the duties of children to their parents, whilst He makes no express mention whatsoever of the duties of parents to their children? Are not the latter as sacred and as binding as the former? They no doubt are. But a plausible answer seems to be given by daily experience. Parents as a rule rather abound than lack in the love they entertain for and tender their children. Their natural parental instinct seems to be a sufficient law unto them. They appear not to need a particular reminder and a solemn challenge to do what they usually find their greatest delight in doing. Not so, however, are the children. They easily forget and often seriously neglect their most natural, sacred and obvious duties of filial love, veneration and thankfulness. Hence the solemn insistence of the decalogue holding children to their obligations.

"Honor" Implies Everything

A further question is, why does the fourth commandment only use the word "honor", without making mention of the duty to love and obey parents? Because honor, when sincerely and thoroughly tendered, implies love and obedience of a high order. There are children who really love their parents yet who thoughtlessly withhold from them the honor that is due them. There are those, too, who obey their parents, and yet neglect to honor them as they should. Whereas the child who exhibits genuine honor to its parents, thereby demonstrates its abiding love and entire submission to them.

(continued on following page)

Single....Unpicked
(continued)

The point being, if you are downcast about being "unpicked", don't be! You have much to learn and it can be very fulfilling! It can also be fun! It really can be!

Get some cookbooks and start planning the meals!

Learn to sew, crochet, arrange flowers, paint, etc.

Join the Legion of Mary, serve others...at home and elsewhere.

Serve the busy mothers with many children....babysit for them, help with their homeschooling.

Be with the children. Read to them, teach them Catechism. There is nothing so beautiful as a young woman who spends herself for the little ones....

Work hard wherever you are at!

But the most important thing is to grow spiritually! If you can go to daily Mass, do it! Pray for your future spouse.

Read good spiritual Catholic books. Go to my book list online at www.finerfem.com. You will find many wonderful suggestions for reading material!

Learn to be happy, even in trying circumstances. This is the very thing that will carry you through when your vocation is in place and the crosses come.

Life is an adventure! Give, give, give to God and He will more than meet you half way! But be on the lookout for what He is trying to teach you. Have an open heart to His Voice. We do this by grace.

We often don't recognize His Voice but if you are doing what it takes, He will lead you to what His Will is for you. And ultimately, that is what will make you happy!

In my little fairy tale story above, I have one sentence that is very important and I didn't expound on: "After I moved back home, life did not go all that smoothly from this point on." My family life was not great. I met discouragement, I was in tears many times, things could look black. It wasn't roses. But I kept seeking and praying...and trying to have peace with it all.

God didn't turn a deaf ear to me. I had to be patient.

Patience is one of the hardest things to learn…and it is something that will have to be practiced all through our lives.

God is not turning a deaf ear to you! Are you kidding? He loves you and has something wonderful in mind for you!

You must get through the lonely times, those times when you feel "unpicked"; and remember....God sees the bigger picture, you don't. Keep that in mind and seek for inner happiness, through the grace of God, in the interim. Work towards getting "better" not "bitter"!

You will be blessed! Believe it!

Single.....Unpicked
by Leane VanderPutten

Do you feel like you have been forgotten, that your life isn't what it should be, that, somehow, you are not good enough because you are still single?

Another friend is getting married. You are happy to be picked as bridesmaid, but really.....all you want is to be the one walking up the aisle in that beautiful white gown! In your heart you feel....unpicked.

Remember the story in the Bible where another Apostle had to be chosen because Judas was gone from the Little Band? Do you know the method they used to pick between the two men, Barsabbas and Matthias? A prayer was said and straws were drawn and whoever had the longest straw was the disciple!

Wow! That's amazing. Such an important job....and a straw is drawn!

"And they gave them lots, and the lot fell upon Matthias, and he was numbered with the eleven apostles." -Douay Rheims

I'm sure Matthias was very happy! But what about Barsabbas? Did God forget about him? Did God not have big plans for him?

Just because Barsabbas was not "picked" in this particular instance did not mean that God loved him less or that he had been overlooked or that He didn't have wonderful plans laid out for him.

How about you? Do you find it very difficult when the ladies around you are getting "picked" and you are not? Does it make you sad that you have not found that "one and only" yet?

Of course! It is hard to wait on Our Lord when it seems like life is passing quickly!

I remember those single days, in the interim, before I was married. I lived in Canada, really in a spiritual desert. I had quit my "important" job and went to live back with my mom and dad who had moved to a small town and bought a gas station. I pumped gas.

I was reading some very good books at the time and I knew in my heart I wanted the noble and wonderful vocation as wife and mother.

But wife and mother to who? Ah, there lay the rub! The town I lived in had about 400 people. And believe me, serious Catholics were hard to find, even in the big cities!

I remembered what my dear mentor and older friend had said to me. "If you want to be a wife and mother, Leane, start now by learning everything you can about that important vocation. Roll up your sleeves and practice cooking, cleaning, sewing, music, art. Read good books on the subject....on parenting, gardening, 'good wife' books, etc."

This is one reason I had left my job in the big city. To me, it was not helping me get to my final goal. No, it was hindering it. No one could understand why I left and went to pump gas. But I had a goal. And part of that goal was being back home helping Mom and Dad.

Now, life did not go all that smoothly from this point on. But circumstances led me to write a dear priest in the U.S. and I asked him what I should do. He told me to come to his Apostolate, help him by working in the office, and he would help me, mentor me, on my journey.

I did this. I was there for eleven months, serving this dear priest's apostolate, going to Mass and Benediction each day. It was a time of spiritual growth. I learned so much about my Faith! And I met my husband, who had also come to serve at this Catholic Shrine.....

(Continued on following page.)

(continued) The Blessedness of Labor

In short, in considering any state or condition, the principal thing is, to take into account the advantages it holds out for securing a holy and pious life, so that we may come safe through all the trials and temptations of this world to our only true home in heaven.

In this view, I do not know any among the ordinary conditions of life as good and desirable as that of a life of service or of daily labor.

A life of labor has always been considered, by spiritual persons, most favorable to the soul. To have nothing which we are obliged to do may seem very fine to our worldliness and love of ease, but it is most dangerous. You know the old saying: "The devil finds work enough for idle hands to do." It is most true. Idleness opens the door for the worst temptations.

Suppose you had pretty much all your time to do what you pleased with, how likely it is that a great part of it would be misused! Habits of idleness would be formed, your time would hang heavy on your hands, and you would not know what to do.

You would seek for amusement: you would soon be altogether taken up with it, and your whole life would become one given up to the world and to wickedness. You would indeed stand a great chance of going straight down to perdition.

The labor of the hands is, then, a source of blessing. It furnishes a great help to spending life in innocence. It fills up our time with holiest industry, while it leaves the soul free to raise itself from time to time to God.

The labor of the hands is not like that of the head. Head work fills the mind, and takes up its attention, but hand work leaves the mind in a great measure free.

St. Anthony was taught this by an angel from heaven. One day when he felt tired by uninterrupted prayer, and unable to continue it, he grieved over it before the Lord, and begged to be instructed how to get over this trouble, which was a hindrance to his salvation. After his prayer he went out of his cell, and saw a person, the exact image of himself, seated at work making mats out of palm leaves. The saint perceived it was an angel who took this form and acted in this manner to make him understand how, by going from work to prayer, and from prayer to work, he could cheerfully and surely work out his salvation.

The old hermits of the desert all understood this. They did not dare to be idle, but made baskets, cultivated the ground, spent all their time in labor or prayer, and so worked out their salvation in the utmost security.

We cannot have the life of these old hermits of the desert over again nowadays, but, outside the wall of the convent, whose life is most like theirs?

That of the good girl who earns her own living at service, or at some other honest employment. She it is who enjoys, more than any others that I know of, the advantages which these old saints coveted so much — who can spend her days in work and prayer, and thus keep off the evil one, and work out her salvation with comparative ease.

Do not then complain of labor, but rejoice, and thank God that He has given you not a life of idleness, but honest and continual labor. It is a very great favor of His love, as you will see, when this body of the flesh falls away, and you stand on the other side of eternity.

The Blessedness of Labor
Rev. George Deshon, 1863

"Why was I not born a lady?" says the poor girl who has to work hard for a living. "There are the ladies, with little or nothing to do, amusing themselves all day, and enjoying all the good things of life, while poor I must drudge the whole blessed day, from early morning till late at night, for a living, and a scant one at that. I wish the Almighty had placed me in some better condition of life than the one I am in!"

My good girl, you who talk in that way, you do not know what you are saying. Instead of complaining of the good God, if your eyes could only be opened to see things as they really are, your heart would leap for joy, and your tongue would praise Him that you have not been made a lady, or anything, but just what you are.

For the truth is, your condition of life is one of the very best in which God could place you, and it is a great privilege for you to be in it rather than in any other.

Let us look into it, and see how this is. I dare say you remember that among almost the first words of the little Catechism, the question is asked: "For what were we created?"

The answer to it is: "To learn to serve and love God in this world in order that we may be happy forever with Him in the next."

Ah, this lets us into the whole secret! We were not created to be rich, to live without work, to live in fine houses, and wear fine clothes, and ride in elegant coaches, and have, what folks are apt to call, a fine time of it.

No, it was for nothing of all this, but to learn to love and serve God during this life, in order to earn heaven, and prepare ourselves to be happy forever with God.

This is the reason why the rich are so often unhappy, in spite of all their money and splendor.

They are just living for riches and pleasure, instead of to please God, and they cannot find any real satisfaction in such a life. God will never let us have any real happiness unless we live in order to please and love Him.

It is true, a rich man or woman can serve God and be happy, but it is difficult, for riches and honors and pleasures steal away the heart, and cause Him to be forgotten. And when God is forgotten what enjoyment can there be of life?

What is over and above our necessary and suitable clothing will bring but little satisfaction. It only feeds an idle vanity, destroys contentment, and fills us with desires for a thousand things that never satisfy us when they are supplied.

We are always the worse for it when we eat or drink much more than is necessary for us; we lose our appetite, our health and our strength, so that the body becomes a burden, and life a misery.

All the money or honor in the world cannot ensure health or contentment of mind.

Then there is death, in the midst of our earthly enjoyments, always staring us in the face. Our friends are cut down around us, and we know not the day or the hour when our turn will come.

But we know very well that when it does come, we must be torn away, whether we will or no, from everything in this world which we have set our hearts upon.

Can we have any enjoyment in such a life as we have here, unless it is grounded on peace with God? Unless we carry out the blessed intentions which God had in creating us, namely, that we should love and serve Him?

And, then, think of that vast eternity which stretches away beyond, after this life is over. How small and mean everything here is in comparison with it! What difference will it make to us when we are once in the presence of God, clothed with glory and honor, with white garments and the palm of victory in our hands, with no sorrows, sighs, or tears to be feared any more forever; — what difference will it make whether we had a little more or a little less on this earth? Why, this whole life will seem a small speck in the grand ocean of eternity.

Tips for Chaste Company-Keeping (con't)

In confessing sins of impurity, remember the following:

I. If you have real mortal sins to confess, then you must tell what you did and how often you did it. A confessor must know the kind of sin (self-abuse, immodest embracing, fornication) and the number of times; otherwise he may not give absolution. This does not mean that you must give a detailed description of your thoughts or acts.

II. If you are confessing sins of impurity and you mean only venial sins (negligence in regard to thoughts, lack of sufficient reason in external acts) or mere temptations (imaginations or feelings that were not willful), then indicate this to the confessor by saying, "I had bad thoughts, but they were not willful" or "I tried to get rid of them." Otherwise he may think you mean mortal sins.

III. If you wish to confess doubtful sins (you doubt about consent, or whether you confessed the matter before), mention your doubt. Strictly speaking, doubtful sins do not have to be confessed, though it is better to do so, unless your confessor decides otherwise. Nor do you have to abstain from Holy Communion when you merely doubt whether you have sinned.

You must be absolutely sure of having committed a mortal sin before you can say that you are not able to go to Communion.

However, you should make an act of perfect contrition which will dispose your soul for the reception of the Sacrament.

IV. If you have difficulties in regard to chastity or if you are inclined to be scrupulous, you should have a regular confessor. His advice will be more valuable since he will know the condition of your soul and the problems you must meet. Trust him, for God commissioned him to be your friend and your soul's guardian. Go to Confession every week or at least once a month.

This will enable you not only to cleanse your soul from sin, but also to correct your faults and keep yourself pleasing to God. It is one of the best means of keeping courtship clean and happy.

Confession heals, confession justifies, confession grants pardon of sin, all hope consists in confession; in confession there is a chance for mercy.
—St. Isidore of Seville

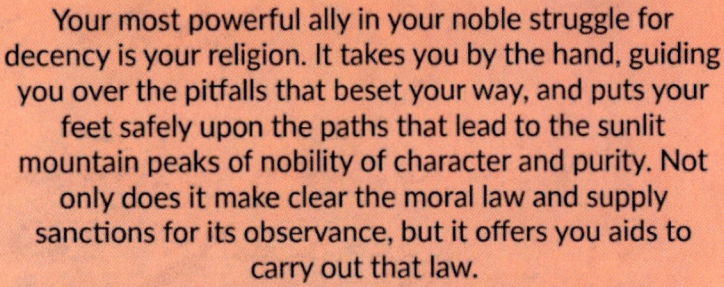

Tips for Chaste Company-Keeping
– Fr. Lawrence Lovasik

Your most powerful ally in your noble struggle for decency is your religion. It takes you by the hand, guiding you over the pitfalls that beset your way, and puts your feet safely upon the paths that lead to the sunlit mountain peaks of nobility of character and purity. Not only does it make clear the moral law and supply sanctions for its observance, but it offers you aids to carry out that law.

While the preservation of purity calls for a constant and determined struggle, you are not struggling single-handedly. God is always ready and willing to help you with His grace. "God is faithful, who will not suffer you to be tempted above that which you are able, but will make also with temptation issue, that you may be able to bear it." (Cor. 10:13.)

With God's all-powerful help, you can win every victory. This grace of God is obtained through the sacraments, prayer, self-denial, and a tender love for Jesus and Mary.

Regular Confession

Regular confession keeps your soul in order. It is God's means of ridding you of and preserving you from the greatest evil in the world—sin. For this reason it is a source of peace and joy.

In the Sacrament of Penance:

I. You receive sanctifying grace if it has been lost by mortal sin (this grace is increased if it had not been lost).

II. Your sins are forgiven.

III. You are freed from eternal punishment due to any mortal sin, and from a part, at least, of the temporal punishment due to your sins.

IV. You receive actual grace, which is God's help to enable you to do good and avoid sin in the future

V. You get back the merits of the good works you have lost by mortal sin. Remember that the most important part of confession is not so much the telling of your sins, as perfect sorrow for them.

Your contrition is perfect when you are sorry because your sins offended God, whom you should love above all things for His own sake. But contrition is also a hatred for the sins you committed, with a firm purpose of sinning no more.

This means that you must really want to make up your mind not to sin any more and to try hard to keep away from whatever leads to sin, such as bad companions, bad places, bad reading.

If you do not really want to keep away from mortal sin and from whatever will surely lead you into it, you make a bad confession.

(continued on next page...)

Frequent Confession (con't)

Mortal Sin

Remember that the commission of a MORTAL SIN requires three things:
1. The nature of the sin must be serious. It must seriously offend God, ourselves or others. If we are not sure whether it is serious we are bound to ask our confessor.
2. We must know what we are doing is a mortal sin at the time we are doing it.
3. We must give full consent. We must freely and deliberately choose to commit the act. Hence, we could not commit a serious sin if we were asleep or partially asleep, or forced to act against our will.

We Cannot Remain Ignorant

It is no use to argue "as long as I did not think it was a mortal sin I did not commit a mortal sin."

God gives us the responsibility of knowing definitely what is mortal and what is not. Anyone who neglects to inform herself on this point is guilty.

Some girls excuse their going with dangerous companions or to places dangerous to their virtue on the grounds "My mother let me." They excuse their wrongdoing with: "I know other Catholic girls who act that way."

We cannot fool God, and we must not try to fool ourselves in matters of conscience. We have the duty to ask our confessor about any doubts we might have concerning the seriousness of our sins.

We cannot pretend that certain things are right when they really are wrong or that certain things are not as bad as God knows them to be. It is important that we learn to judge our sins as God judges them.

Good Effects

Each time we make a good examination of conscience, we see more clearly the weaknesses of our own particular human nature. How often our duties toward God and our fellow man are neglected because we never think of them.

Our conscience is not awake to them. Thus duties which are new to us are disclosed and we are moved to beg God earnestly for the supernatural help we need to perform them well.

Christian joy is a gift of God flowing from a good conscience.
~St. Philip Neri

Frequent Confession
by Rev. Leo F. Griffin, 1945

What makes it so difficult for us to get along with others? What causes so much of our unhappiness? Generally the answer is our venial sins. We can gradually and completely rid ourselves of all deliberate venial sins by making frequent and earnest use of the Sacrament of Penance.

In frequent confession we come to learn that our venial sins are not to be regarded as though they do not matter very much.

They actually pave the way for the commission of mortal sins. Therefore, they must become a matter of concern for every good, Catholic girl.

We can lessen the intensity and duration of our Purgatory by frequent confession. Moreover, the grace of this Sacrament is poured into our lives.

Thus we acquire a steady stream of spiritual help in overcoming our fault.

We are given additional strength against some powerful temptation which could suddenly rise up and overcome us.

Finally, because of the constant help we receive in confession, we can do more easily the difficult things our Catholic life requires of us.

In Praise of Unmarried Women (con't)
GREAT CONTRIBUTION

Their contribution to the early Church is beyond computation. They lived the purity that was supposed to characterize the religion of the Savior. They did the good works that He had listed as sign and proof of His followers.

They were personally the great correctives for the abuses of marriage and for the corruption of morals. They demonstrated with shining and spectacular force that it was possible for married couples to remain faithful since normal girls with all the normal desires and impulses could remain pure while unmarried.

They led along paths of maidenly modesty other girls who could not accept a lifetime of virginity, until premarital purity made them worthy to be mothers of the little sons and daughters of our God and Father. The Church has never forgotten those first unmarried saints, the models of the millions who were to be the most distinctive and unique contribution of Christianity to world morality. Christian marriage would never have been possible without them. Christian virginity got its pattern from their unforgettable acceptance of Christ's new purity.

It is not at all an exaggeration to say that the unmarried Catholic woman of the present can look upon herself as the legitimate successor to these virgins and martyrs of earliest Christian times. She may be proud of that association and conscious of the possibility within her to repeat in our generation their great contribution to life, love, and the decencies.

REWARD

No doubt about it, the unmarried woman has the chance to win a reward exceeding great.

She is able daily to offer to God the beautiful perfume that is her virginal innocence. God loves her for that and honors her with the same kind of reverence that is due Mary. So do those of His followers who see life and measure values with a Christ-like eye.

If the cup of cold water given in Christ's name wins eternal reward, what of the food and drink and clothes and housing that are provided by these generous women again and again and again?

May this saintly woman come very close to God. For there is no interfering love in her life. Those she loves, she loves unselfishly, almost without human reward but in the calm certainty that God is pleased by her life. "Whatsoever you do for the least of these my little ones, you do for me."

The words of the Savior, tremendously reassuring, never fitted anyone more perfectly than they do Catholic teachers, Catholic nurses, Catholic businesswomen, and those sisters, daughters, and aunts who do and do and do – endlessly and without probability of repayment – for the sons and daughters of others – and of God.

The fine Catholic example of this kind of women has far more influence than she herself dreams.

Her laborious unselfishness is a constant rebuke to the greed and self-indulgence of the world. She is one of those unrecognized heroines whose work is never properly praised but is always effective to a degree that will be measured by celestial weights and measures.

She is not an unworthy successor of the holy women of the primitive Church who, with the Apostles and the doctors of the Church, taught a new way of life to humanity.

VISION

Nor can we forget the bright and inspiring vision of St. John. There upon the mount that is Sion he saw the Lamb of God surrounded by the specially honored one hundred and forty-four thousand, a mystical number embracing the vast host of those who will be nearest the Savior in eternity. Their closeness to the Savior, Saint John explains by one simple statement: "For they are virgins." (See Rev 14:4)

Lift up your eyes, you heroines called spinsters! The Savior of the world loves you most especially and has a place for you in eternity in His own immediate company. It is a glorious certainty.

And if a certain group of spinsters will permit me to bring them back from those sublime heights to a more immediately grateful person . . . I thank you . . . and you . . . and you . . . and you . . . and all you others with whom it has been my happy privilege to be associated in a common enterprise during these many years. I know your holiness. I have felt your unselfishness. I know your shining beauty.

Surely my life has been made rich and full by the fact that I have counted you among my friends and partners in a work for the unmarried Christ and the Virgin Mary.

In Praise of Unmarried Women
by REV. DANIEL A. LORD, S.J.
Australian Catholic Truth Society 1950

Whatever literature may say about spinsters, and however much history may ignore them – except for outstanding spinsters like Elizabeth of England – the Church's attitude toward unmarried women has been, from the first, one of reverence.

This I came to know when my faith emerged from mere youthful practice to intelligent study and appreciation. Among the Jews a spinster was merely an unfortunate girl not lucky enough to have won a husband for herself. Among the pagans she was usually the slave or bondmaiden, the grudgingly tolerated hanger-on in the house of her parents or her luckier married sisters.

With St. Paul all that was changed. He loved virginity, and he turned to the ministrations and loyalty – as many a parish has done since – of the splendid young and older unmarried women of his time. The legends of St. Paul and St. Tecla – whose name was the Greek word for pearl – are many and beautiful. Phoebe, to whom Paul sends affectionate messages, seems to have been one of the first consecrated Catholic virgins.

ST. PAUL SPEAKS

It was left for the great St. Paul, who could find for marriage no more appropriate comparison than that of the love which Christ bears for His Church (see Ephesians 5: 21-32), to speak almost the first words in praise of those who deliberately did not marry or who, for any good reasons, remained unmarried.

"But," he wrote to the Corinthians, "I say to the unmarried and to widows, it is good for them if they so remain, even as I." (1 Cor 7: 8)

Then he directs to men who remain unmarried and cherish their virginity strong praise that quite clearly he means for both men and women. For he continues: "I would have you free from care. He who is unmarried is concerned about the things of the Lord, how he may please God. Whereas he who is married is concerned about the things of the world, how he may please his wife; and he is divided. And the unmarried woman, and the virgin, thinks about the things of the Lord, that she may be holy in body and in spirit. Whereas she who is married thinks about the things of the world, how she may please her husband." (1 Cor 7: 32-34)

UNMARRIED SAINTS

This was an astonishing teaching to people who had regarded virginity as rather a futile thing and the unmarried girl as the object of a none too gentle pity. Yet instantly the early Church, which loved the virgin Christ and the Virgin Mary and the beloved virgin John, took to heart the good advice. It is noteworthy that the virgin martyrs of those early days were not nuns in any modern sense. They had in some cases taken the veil of virginity at the hands of Peter or of Paul, but they lived at home, served the poor in the big cities, and, save for their intense concentration on the love of God and their neighbors, lived, as we would say, in the world.

Such was the young Agnes, the older Agatha, Cecilia, and half a dozen others forced into marriage against their will and carrying to God through martyrdom the glory of their virginity. They had detached themselves from the love of any man to give their whole love to the greatest of the sons of men.

They cared for their houses and were devoted to their parents. They ministered to the poor and at dawn or at dusk went to the catacombs for Mass and prayer. They were saintly spinsters, if you wish, or spinster saints. True, the pagan world regarded them as abnormal and queer and fit only for death. The Christians loved them unforgettably.

(continued on next page)

WHAT DO YOU MEAN, BEAUTY? (con't)

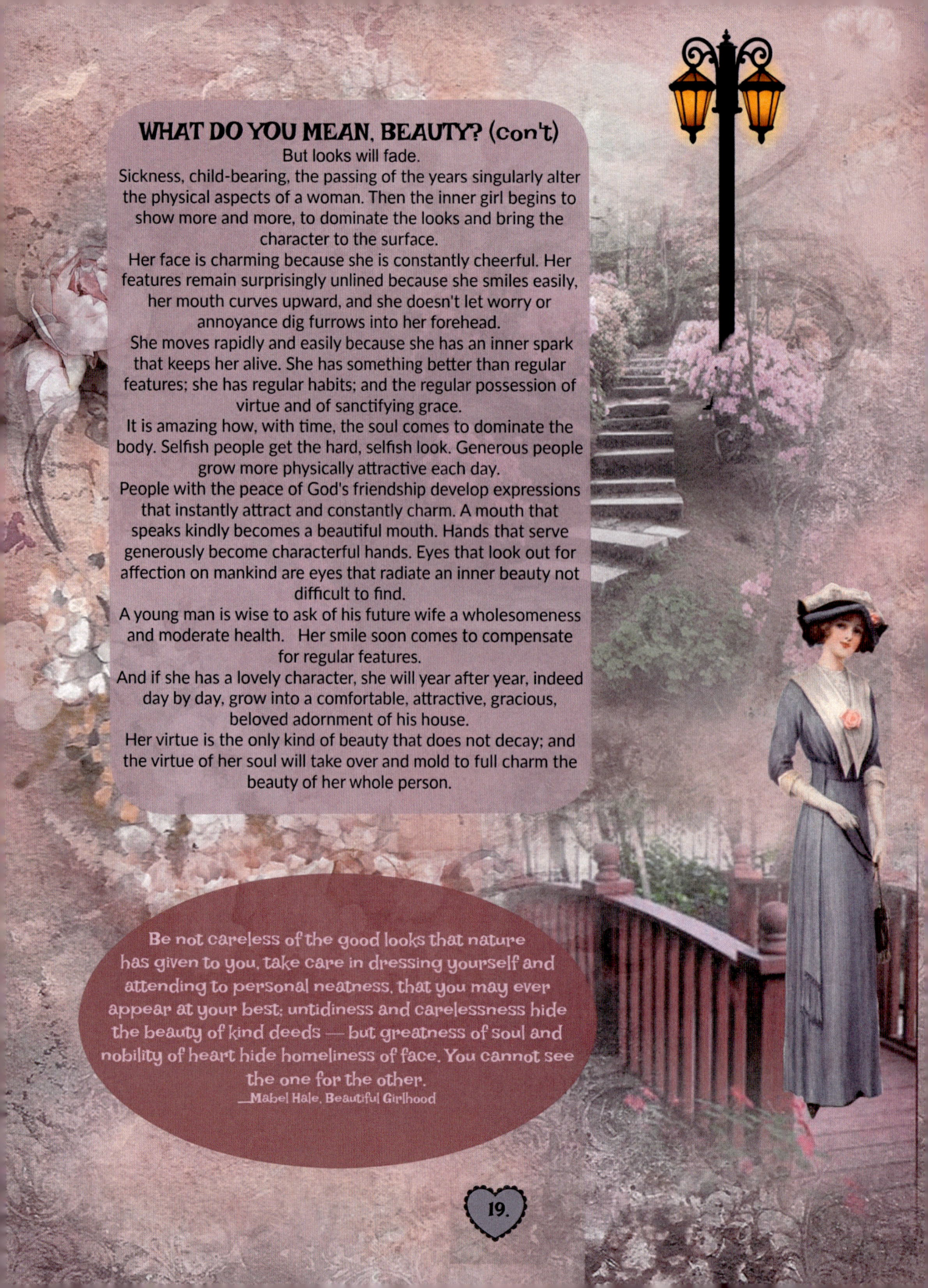

But looks will fade.

Sickness, child-bearing, the passing of the years singularly alter the physical aspects of a woman. Then the inner girl begins to show more and more, to dominate the looks and bring the character to the surface.

Her face is charming because she is constantly cheerful. Her features remain surprisingly unlined because she smiles easily, her mouth curves upward, and she doesn't let worry or annoyance dig furrows into her forehead.

She moves rapidly and easily because she has an inner spark that keeps her alive. She has something better than regular features; she has regular habits; and the regular possession of virtue and of sanctifying grace.

It is amazing how, with time, the soul comes to dominate the body. Selfish people get the hard, selfish look. Generous people grow more physically attractive each day.

People with the peace of God's friendship develop expressions that instantly attract and constantly charm. A mouth that speaks kindly becomes a beautiful mouth. Hands that serve generously become characterful hands. Eyes that look out for affection on mankind are eyes that radiate an inner beauty not difficult to find.

A young man is wise to ask of his future wife a wholesomeness and moderate health. Her smile soon comes to compensate for regular features.

And if she has a lovely character, she will year after year, indeed day by day, grow into a comfortable, attractive, gracious, beloved adornment of his house.

Her virtue is the only kind of beauty that does not decay; and the virtue of her soul will take over and mold to full charm the beauty of her whole person.

Be not careless of the good looks that nature has given to you, take care in dressing yourself and attending to personal neatness, that you may ever appear at your best; untidiness and carelessness hide the beauty of kind deeds — but greatness of soul and nobility of heart hide homeliness of face. You cannot see the one for the other.
—Mabel Hale, Beautiful Girlhood

WHAT DO YOU MEAN, BEAUTY?
Rev. Daniel A. Lord

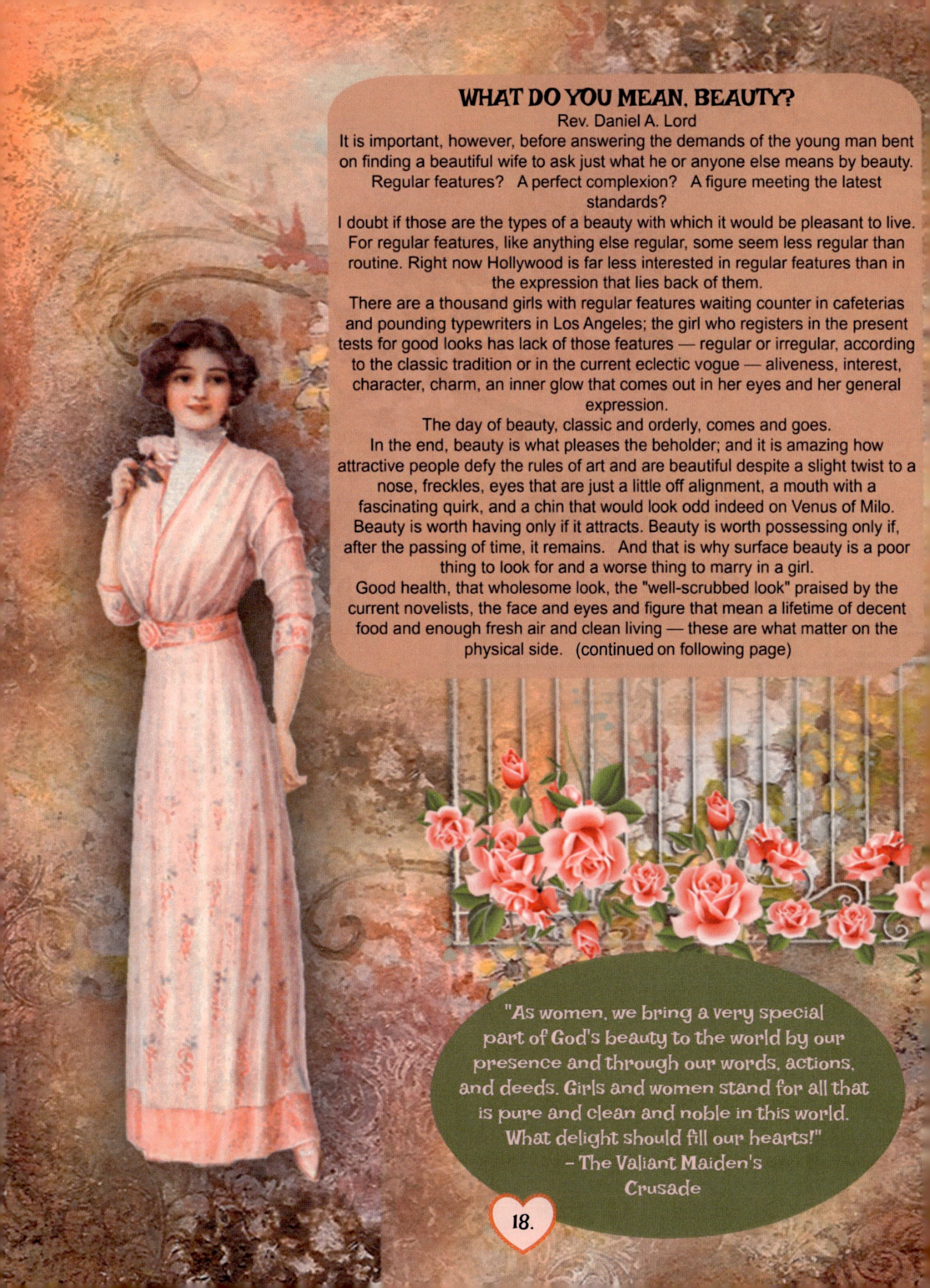

It is important, however, before answering the demands of the young man bent on finding a beautiful wife to ask just what he or anyone else means by beauty. Regular features? A perfect complexion? A figure meeting the latest standards?

I doubt if those are the types of a beauty with which it would be pleasant to live. For regular features, like anything else regular, some seem less regular than routine. Right now Hollywood is far less interested in regular features than in the expression that lies back of them.

There are a thousand girls with regular features waiting counter in cafeterias and pounding typewriters in Los Angeles; the girl who registers in the present tests for good looks has lack of those features — regular or irregular, according to the classic tradition or in the current eclectic vogue — aliveness, interest, character, charm, an inner glow that comes out in her eyes and her general expression.

The day of beauty, classic and orderly, comes and goes.

In the end, beauty is what pleases the beholder; and it is amazing how attractive people defy the rules of art and are beautiful despite a slight twist to a nose, freckles, eyes that are just a little off alignment, a mouth with a fascinating quirk, and a chin that would look odd indeed on Venus of Milo.

Beauty is worth having only if it attracts. Beauty is worth possessing only if, after the passing of time, it remains. And that is why surface beauty is a poor thing to look for and a worse thing to marry in a girl.

Good health, that wholesome look, the "well-scrubbed look" praised by the current novelists, the face and eyes and figure that mean a lifetime of decent food and enough fresh air and clean living — these are what matter on the physical side. (continued on following page)

"As women, we bring a very special part of God's beauty to the world by our presence and through our words, actions, and deeds. Girls and women stand for all that is pure and clean and noble in this world. What delight should fill our hearts!"
– The Valiant Maiden's Crusade

18.

When is Kissing a Sin?
Fr. Donald Miller, C.SS.R., 1950's

Problem:
Is kissing a sin?

Solution:
Almost wherever there are young people who go out on dates, this question is posed to those who take an interest in their welfare both spiritual and temporal. It is obvious that the customs and fashions of the world in which they live have made it a serious problem that must be faced.

In answering it, we shall consider the moral angle first, and then add considerations of prudence and common sense. There are two different kinds of kissing that can be referred to in the question.

The first is the ordinary kiss of greeting and farewell, the kiss that people are not ashamed to give in public or in the presence of others, the kind of kiss exchanged between a mother and son, brother and sister, relative and relative.

It is a salutation, a symbol, a sign of love and respect for a person to whom one is bound by the more sacred ties of human relationship. Clearly this kind of kissing is not sinful, not sinful even between a boy and girl in love.

Usually when this much has been explained, young people answer rather scornfully: "Oh, we don't mean that kind of kissing."

Or they will cry out with still greater scorn: "How can you expect us to kiss like a brother and sister if we are in love?" This is very revealing.

It means that what such young people have in mind when they ask "Is kissing a sin?" is not the mere symbol or salutation of affection, but something inspired by and bound up in some way with passion.

They are referring to close and protracted embraces; the kisses that gratify, in some way, the yearning for bodily union with another that can lawfully be fulfilled only in marriage. Sometimes they do not realize that this is the origin of their desire for protracted kissing experiences, but the fact remains that it is just that, and in many cases it leads them straight into the great sins that beforehand they would have said they abhorred.

That is why such kissing, prolonged, passionate, exciting, is a sin in itself. It is a sin in so far as it springs from and leads to indulgence in sinful passion.

On the prudential side, even the kisses that are merely symbols of affection should not be made common, cheap and promiscuous. Kisses should be reserved for the more strong and sacred relationships in life. The boy and girl who make them cheap will almost invariably cheapen even nobler and more important things.

"A desire to be beautiful is not unwomanly. A woman who is not beautiful cannot properly fill her place. But, mark you, true beauty is not of the face, but of the soul. There is a beauty so deep and lasting that it will shine out of the homeliest face and make it comely. This is the beauty to be first sought and admired. It is a quality of the mind and heart and is manifested in word and deed."
- Beautiful Girlhood, Mabel Hale

The HEART MAKES the life. A beautiful soul will make even a homely face BEAUTIFUL. Seek, dear girls, to be "all glorious within."
-J.R. Miller

Finer Femininity

Quotes...

"Devote yourself to your labor as well as to the fulfillment of all your duties energetically and with a pure intention to please God and make yourself useful to your neighbor. Raise your heart to God from time to time by means of fervent ejaculations (short, quick prayers to heaven), that it may not be narrowed by earthly occupations."
- Fr. Lasance,
My Prayer Book

"The desired wife has developed her personality before marriage and continues that development during marriage. By personality here I mean beauty of soul and all those qualities and accomplishments which go to make a person interesting and sought after. Personality will carry a girl a great deal further in life than physical beauty. In fact, without personality, beauty often tires one in married life. Some girls are born with physical beauty. None are born with personality. They must develop and cultivate it all the days of their lives."
- Fr. Leo Kinsella

"Being humble means recognizing everything good and beautiful in my life (my qualities, the good I can do, and so on), as a gift from God." - Fr. Jacques Philippe, The Way of Trust and Love

"How beautiful is the religious life! Just as Jesus once met young people in His day and said, 'Come, follow me!' so He says the same thing to your children today, at home, at school, or at work. It is really the most wonderful life that your teenagers could choose for themselves."
-Fr. Lawrence G. Lovasik. The Catholic Family Handbook

"A young woman who prevails on her fiancé to approach the Sacraments with her at regular intervals builds up a strong bulwark against improper advances and obtains the best guarantee for a happy future. True love gives strength of character and assists in the acquisition of self-control. It never takes advantage of another for the sake of personal gratification. Good and pure-minded women inspire respect and make the task of a young man easy, for he will have no difficulty in keeping the right distance."
– Fr. Lovasik,
Clean Love in
Courtship

More Fun!

HATS FOR THE LADIES
Decorate straw hats with silk flowers and beautiful ribbons. Wear your hats for tea— and be sure to pose for an elegant group picture.

DO-IT-YOURSELF CHINA
At a discount or thrift store, buy plain white or glass plates. Give one to each of your guests and then have everyone use glass or china paints (you can get them at craft stores) and tiny paintbrushes to decorate their plates with a sweet design.

BROKEN CUPS
Before the party, draw a pretty teacup for each guest. Make sure to include on each cup a special message like "Thanks for being my friend!" or "I'm so glad you came." Then cut each drawing into eight or ten pieces that aren't too easy to put back together. Put the pieces of each drawing into pretty envelopes (one set of teacup pieces per envelope) and give an envelope to each guest as she arrives. Then, sometime during the party, have your guests assemble their cups (" On your mark, get set, go!"). The first one who puts her broken cup back together is the winner.

TEATIME MEMORY TEASER
Bring out a tray on which you have put a number of well-known tea objects like a teacup, teabags, a tea strainer, a sugar bowl, milk, a lemon, and baked goodies. Bring out the tray and let your guests look at it for a full minute. Then take the tray away and give each person a pencil, a piece of paper, and three minutes to write down everything she saw on the tray. Remember, the more items you put on the tray, the more you tease the memory! Have a special gift ready for the person who remembers the greatest number of objects. You could let that person choose something from the tray.

Menu
Angel Food Cake with Strawberries & Cream, Cucumber Tea Sandwiches, Chocolate-Dipped Strawberries, Tea with Rosehips or Fruit Punch

Angel Food Cake with Strawberries and Cream
1 Angel Food cake (purchased or homemade)
2 pints of fresh strawberries
¼ cup of sugar
1 container of whipped topping

Wash the strawberries. Cut off the green stem and leaves. Then slice the strawberries. Sprinkle them with sugar and set them aside. Next, with a long knife (and an adult's help), slice the cake horizontally twice so that you have three layers.

Now brush the loose crumbs off each layer and place the bottom layer on a pretty plate. Spread the top of the layer with whipped topping and then cover it with strawberry slices. Place the second layer on top of the bottom one. Spread the top of this layer with whipped topping and strawberry slices. Now place the top layer on the cake and frost the entire cake with the rest of the whipped topping. Decorate the cake with the strawberries you have left. Store the cake in the refrigerator until it's time for tea.

Cucumber Tea Sandwiches
Cucumbers
White bread
Whipped cream cheese
Unsalted butter, softened
Salt

Peel the cucumbers and slice them very thin. Sprinkle the slices with salt and then put them on paper towels to drain. For each sandwich, spread a little bit of cream cheese on two slices of bread. Then layer the cucumber slices on one piece of bread, but don't stack them higher than ¼ inch. Now cut them into square tea sandwiches.

Chocolate-Dipped Strawberries
Whole fresh strawberries, washed and dried Semisweet chocolate chips.

Fill a small deep container (like a coffee cup) with chocolate chips and place it in the microwave. To melt the chocolate, heat it on high for 20 seconds, open the microwave and stir the chocolate, and then heat it again for 20 more seconds. Continue heating the chocolate at 20-second intervals until it is just melted. Then hold a strawberry by its broad top and dip the bottom part of the berry into the melted chocolate. Set the strawberry on wax paper to cool. Continue dipping until you've dipped all the strawberries. Store the dipped berries in the refrigerator.

A Tea Party!
—Emilie Barnes

Do you have a special friend— someone to laugh with and share secrets with? Someone to run with, play with, and just hang out with? Someone who knows what you're thinking before you say anything? Well, one of my special friends is named Christine, and she just had a birthday. To celebrate that important day, we had a traditional and very elegant Victorian high tea. You know, the kind where tea is served in china cups and stirred with silver spoons. The kind of tea where very proper ladies wear white gloves and hold their little finger in the air when they sip their tea. It was the kind of pretty party every girl dreams of. Here are some ideas for a party you could give for one of your special friends.

Invitations

First find some lovely white paper or printed-border note cards. Then use your fanciest handwriting to write invitations. Let your guests know when and where the party is and ask them to wear their dressi-est clothes and to bring a pretty teacup to use.

An Elegant Table

For many years, hostesses have used a lovely white cloth made out of linen or crisp cotton for their fancy tea parties. You will also need white linen or cotton napkins. Silver napkin rings would be elegant, but you might want to tie satin ribbons around the napkins instead. Large gold or silver doilies make beautiful placemats. Then, for the centerpiece, you might use a fresh bouquet of roses and greenery, but daisies and baby breath are also nice. Pretty serving pieces like china plates, silver trays, and Grandma's teapot or cut-glass punchbowl would be special touches.

Serving Tea the Proper Way

Begin by asking each of your guests if she wants cream or sugar in her tea. Pour the cream into the cup first. Add sugar cubes next, one lump or two (or more) according to your guest's request. Finally, carefully pour the tea into the cup. Make sure you provide a spoon for stirring and a saucer to put under the cup. And always be sure to use your nicest manners at a Tea Party.

Dating Non-Catholics
(continued)

As your child grows older, his relationship with God, his point of view on life and its problems, his conduct will deepen on what he learned in his own home. Both parents in a mixed marriage promise to see that the child is made into a good Christian. But how often does the non-Catholic sit by complacently while his boy or girl is taught to view Christ through Catholic eyes only? Can you easily teach him that the Catholic Church is Christ in the world today?

What about Catholic worship? We participate in the sacrifice of the Body and Blood of Christ to our heavenly Father daily, and weekly under pain of sin.

Can a child of a mixed marriage embrace this mystery and this worship, if either Pop or Mom never goes to Mass? How can your son, for example, learn how important it is to acknowledge the supremacy of God, if your spouse indicates that morning and night prayers are unnecessary?

Being brought up as a Catholic, he'll often ask one or both of you to hear his Catechism lessons. Will your partner help your child to learn principles which may conflict with those cherished by non-Catholics? These are just a few of the sticky situations which repeatedly arise in a mixed marriage.

Have you fond memories of how your parents celebrated the great feast days like Christmas and Easter? Most people do. As a parent, you want to give the same happy memories to your children. In many families, for instance, parents and children attend early Christmas Mass and receive Holy Communion together. This practice unites the family on this great feast day.

But when the parents have different religions, the mother may go to one church and the father to another. The family is separated at the very moment it should be together. And it is togetherness on basic things that really makes a family. Separateness does not belong in the home.

> Love, courtship and marriage are part of a divine plan. The flame of love that burns in the bosom of sweethearts is kindled by no human hands, but by a spark from the love that is eternal and divine.
>
> It is God's perfect gift to man.
> –Fr. Lovasik

Dating Non-Catholics
Rev. George A. Kelly

Fourteen-year-old Pete was talking to his freshman pal, "I don't know why the Church keeps harping on mixed marriages," he said. "I know Protestant girls who are just as nice as Catholic ones. What's wrong with marrying one?"

Pete's argument isn't unusual. Many other Catholics – adults as well as teen-agers – have the same view. They know non-Catholics who obey God's laws and who are decent, respectable grownups.

We all probably know Protestants and Jews who are a greater credit to their religion than some who claim to be Catholics. So why does the Church continually warn against marrying them?

If the problem were as simple as Pete thinks, the teachings of the Church would have no justification. But this is one of those cases I spoke of earlier – a case where you should consider the experience of older people.

Against the fourteen years Pete has to support his viewpoint, the Church has almost two thousand years plus the opportunity to study the results of millions of marriages.

Surely she knows more about this subject than anyone. And she has found that the Catholic entering a mixed marriage takes a terrible chance of going to hell for eternity, and of going through a hell on earth in the meantime.

Suppose you're married to a non-Catholic. What's life like?

You and your mate hold conflicting ideas over the most basic beliefs of your existence. Frequently, there is little agreement on what life is all about – why you were born, what kind of life you're supposed to lead on earth, what you are supposed to do in marriage, what will happen to you after you die.

On these, the most important questions in your life, your non-Catholic partner has been taught beliefs different from the ones you hold.

Other differences arise almost every day of your life.

You must abstain from meat on Friday in memory of Our Lord's sacrifice in giving His life for mankind. Your non-Catholic partner thinks your practice is silly.

You want to arise early on Sunday to attend Mass. Your partner urges you to roll over and go back to sleep.

It sometimes calls for great sacrifice on your part to go to confession and receive Holy Communion. Instead of encouraging such sacrifices, your partner by word and deed indicates that they're totally unnecessary.

When your children are born, your problems multiply. When you were married in the Church, your partner solemnly agreed to bring up the children as Catholics. But this promise is much harder to keep than to make.

For instance, the baby must receive a saint's name. Your mate wants to name him after a favorite uncle. It's a major irritation when that can't be done. (Continued on following page.)

Are You Beautiful? (con't)

At last the teacher spoke. "To my mind Jennie Higgins has the most beautiful hands of any girl in school," she said quietly.

"Jennie Higgins!" exclaimed Nettie in amazement; "Why, her hands are rough and red and look as if she took no care of them. I never thought of them as beautiful."

"I have seen those hands carrying dainty food to the sick, and soothing the brow of the aged. She is her widowed mother's main help, and she it is who does the milking and carries the wood and water, yes, and washes dishes night and morning, that her mother may be saved the hard work. I have never known her to be too tired to speak kindly to her little sister and help her in her play. I have found those busy hands helping her brother with his kite. I tell you I think they are the most beautiful hands I have ever seen, for they are always busy helping somewhere."

This is the beauty for which every girl should strive — the beauty that comes from unselfishness and usefulness. Beauty of face and form is secondary in importance, though not to be despised. If used properly, personal beauty is a good gift; but if it turns a girl's head it becomes a curse to her.

Think of such women as are much spoken of through the public press, or who have achieved noble deeds, as Frances Willard, Florence Nightingale, or Edith Cavell, and consider whether you ever heard if they were pretty or not. No one ever thinks of such trifles when speaking of those who are great of soul.

The girl who depends on her pretty face or form for attraction is to be pitied. Those articles in magazines that so exalt the idea of personal beauty are pandering to the lower part of nature. One may be perfectly beautiful so far as that kind of beauty goes, and lack to as great an extent that true beauty which is like a royal diadem upon the head.

Those who give much time to increasing their personal charms are living on a lower level than is altogether becoming to womanhood. A beautiful soul shining out of a homely face is far more attractive than a beautiful face out of which looks a soul full of selfishness and coldness.

Be not careless of the good looks that nature has given to you, take care in dressing yourself and attending to personal neatness, that you may ever appear at your best; untidiness and carelessness hide the beauty of kind deeds — but greatness of soul and nobility of heart hide homeliness of face. You cannot see the one for the other.

Seek goodness and purity first, then strive to keep the body in harmony with the beauty of the heart. Take time to make yourself presentable, but do not use the time before your glass that should be given to loving service. Let your chief charm be of heart and spirit, not of face and form. Seek the true beauty which lasts even into old age.

Solomon, in one of his wise sayings, expressed plainly the evil that comes to a woman who is beautiful of face but lacks the true beauty of soul. "As a jewel of gold in a swine's snout, so is a fair woman which is without discretion." [Proverbs 11:22]

As the swine would plunge the golden jewel into the filth and the mire as he dug in the dirt, so will a pretty woman who is not good drag her beauty down to the very lowest. There are many peculiar temptations to those who are only fair of face. Without true beauty of soul a pretty face is a dangerous gift.

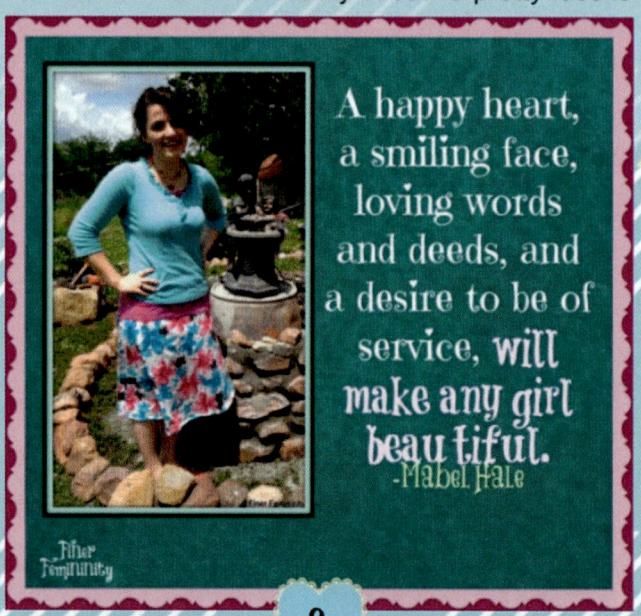

A happy heart, a smiling face, loving words and deeds, and a desire to be of service, will make any girl beautiful.
-Mabel Hale

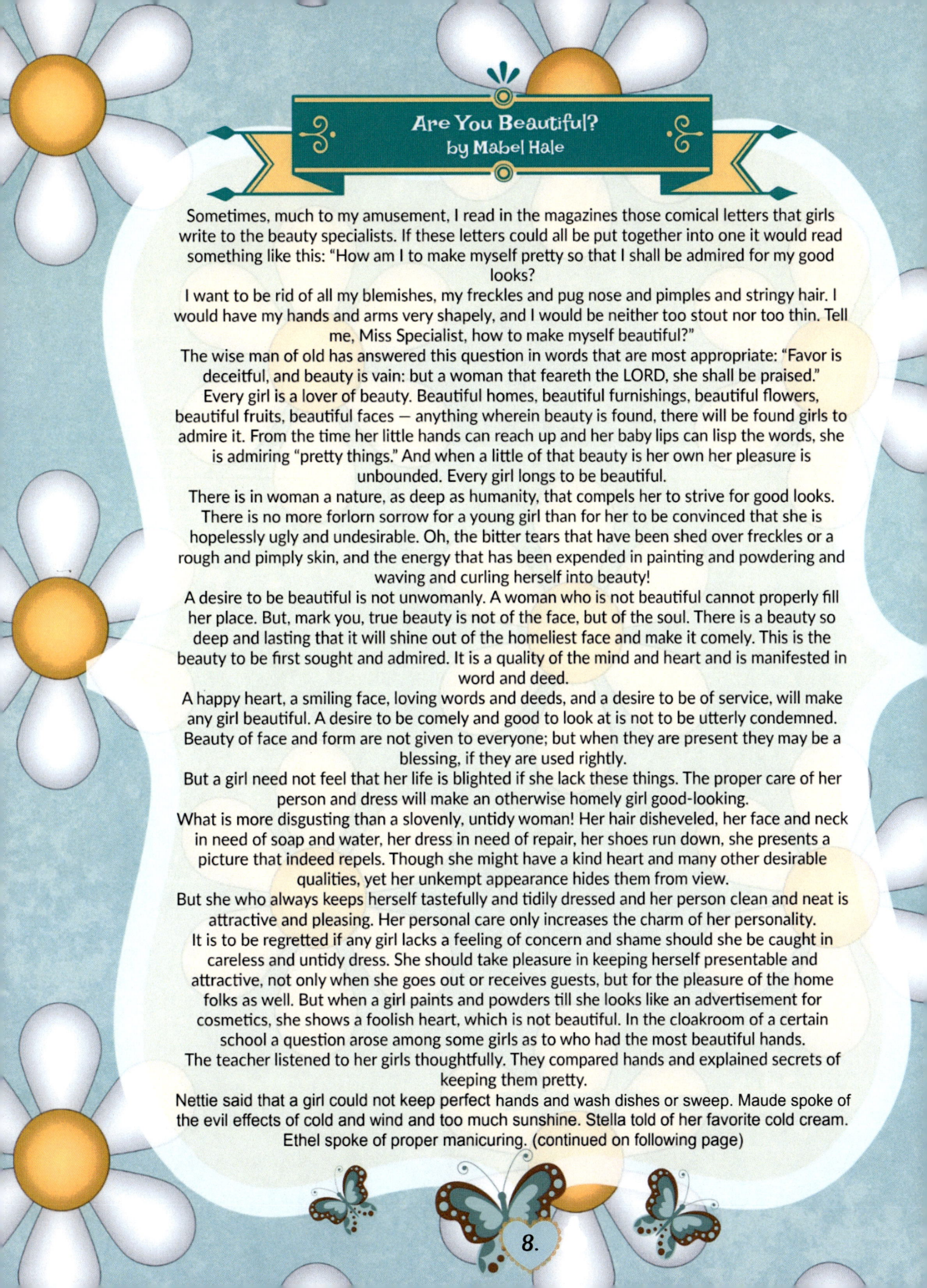

Are You Beautiful?
by Mabel Hale

Sometimes, much to my amusement, I read in the magazines those comical letters that girls write to the beauty specialists. If these letters could all be put together into one it would read something like this: "How am I to make myself pretty so that I shall be admired for my good looks?

I want to be rid of all my blemishes, my freckles and pug nose and pimples and stringy hair. I would have my hands and arms very shapely, and I would be neither too stout nor too thin. Tell me, Miss Specialist, how to make myself beautiful?"

The wise man of old has answered this question in words that are most appropriate: "Favor is deceitful, and beauty is vain: but a woman that feareth the LORD, she shall be praised."

Every girl is a lover of beauty. Beautiful homes, beautiful furnishings, beautiful flowers, beautiful fruits, beautiful faces — anything wherein beauty is found, there will be found girls to admire it. From the time her little hands can reach up and her baby lips can lisp the words, she is admiring "pretty things." And when a little of that beauty is her own her pleasure is unbounded. Every girl longs to be beautiful.

There is in woman a nature, as deep as humanity, that compels her to strive for good looks. There is no more forlorn sorrow for a young girl than for her to be convinced that she is hopelessly ugly and undesirable. Oh, the bitter tears that have been shed over freckles or a rough and pimply skin, and the energy that has been expended in painting and powdering and waving and curling herself into beauty!

A desire to be beautiful is not unwomanly. A woman who is not beautiful cannot properly fill her place. But, mark you, true beauty is not of the face, but of the soul. There is a beauty so deep and lasting that it will shine out of the homeliest face and make it comely. This is the beauty to be first sought and admired. It is a quality of the mind and heart and is manifested in word and deed.

A happy heart, a smiling face, loving words and deeds, and a desire to be of service, will make any girl beautiful. A desire to be comely and good to look at is not to be utterly condemned. Beauty of face and form are not given to everyone; but when they are present they may be a blessing, if they are used rightly.

But a girl need not feel that her life is blighted if she lack these things. The proper care of her person and dress will make an otherwise homely girl good-looking.

What is more disgusting than a slovenly, untidy woman! Her hair disheveled, her face and neck in need of soap and water, her dress in need of repair, her shoes run down, she presents a picture that indeed repels. Though she might have a kind heart and many other desirable qualities, yet her unkempt appearance hides them from view.

But she who always keeps herself tastefully and tidily dressed and her person clean and neat is attractive and pleasing. Her personal care only increases the charm of her personality.

It is to be regretted if any girl lacks a feeling of concern and shame should she be caught in careless and untidy dress. She should take pleasure in keeping herself presentable and attractive, not only when she goes out or receives guests, but for the pleasure of the home folks as well. But when a girl paints and powders till she looks like an advertisement for cosmetics, she shows a foolish heart, which is not beautiful. In the cloakroom of a certain school a question arose among some girls as to who had the most beautiful hands.

The teacher listened to her girls thoughtfully. They compared hands and explained secrets of keeping them pretty.

Nettie said that a girl could not keep perfect hands and wash dishes or sweep. Maude spoke of the evil effects of cold and wind and too much sunshine. Stella told of her favorite cold cream. Ethel spoke of proper manicuring. (continued on following page)

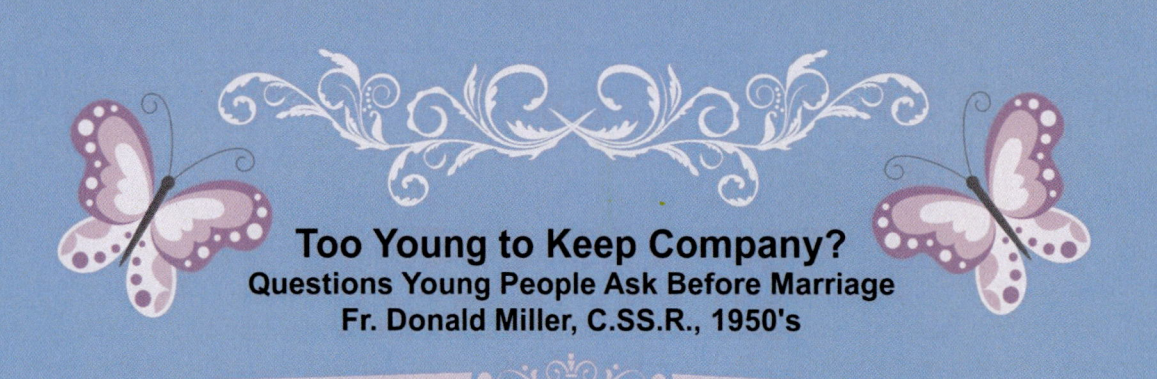

Too Young to Keep Company?
Questions Young People Ask Before Marriage
Fr. Donald Miller, C.SS.R., 1950's

Problem:

I am 14 years old, a sophomore in high school, and I have a boy friend who is 16. We go out together twice a week, sometimes more often. My mother tells me I'm too young to be keeping company like that, but all the kids are doing it. I can't see that there is anything wrong with it. Is there?

Solution:

Our answer to the above question must be directed chiefly to 14, 15, and 16 year-old high school girls who have not yet gone in for company keeping. (There are many such, despite our correspondent's statement about "all the kids.")

It is our sad experience that there is little use in talking to very young girls who already have their "steady" boy friends.

Keeping company makes them feel wise beyond their years. Because they are acting as if they were adults by this practice, they usually feel that they have a right to talk back to adults who tell them it is unwise, dangerous, and harmful to their later lives.

We hope our correspondent is an exception, though the way she tosses aside her mother's advice would indicate otherwise.

Steady company keeping is only for those who have a right to think about marrying within a reasonable time; who are free from responsibilities that company keeping would interfere with; and who are mature enough to recognize and resist the dangers that go with company keeping.

A 14 or 15 year-old girl in high school fulfills none of these conditions. She shouldn't and ordinarily doesn't want to think of getting married for a good number of years.

She should be occupied with the business of getting an education, and nothing can so thoroughly nullify her efforts in that regard as the excitement of puppy love and the time wasted on frequent dates.

Above all, she is too young to be aware of the danger of sin that is inherent in her own nature and that may be presented by her equally immature boy friend in the close associations of adolescent company keeping.

There is great need of a corps of young people of high school age who will resist the all too common practice of regular dating and steady company keeping.

Such young people must be humble enough to realize that their elders are not talking through their hats nor adopting the roll of kill-joys when they advise against the practice. They must know that while again America makes light of it, true Christian principle condemns it.

"True love isn't expressed in passionately whispered words, an intimate kiss or an embrace; before two people are married, love is expressed in self-control, patience, even words left unsaid."

–Joshua Harris

Courtship Prayer

Remember, O Most Blessed Mother, that never was it known that anyone who fled to thy protection, implored thy help, or sought thy intercession, was left unaided. Inspired with this confidence, unworthy as I am of thy protection, in the presence of God the Father, the Author of Life, of God the Son, Who gave marriage the dignity of a sacrament, of God the Holy Ghost, Who sanctified marital love, I entrust my courtship to thy motherly protection. Guide me in the choice of a partner. Keep my courtship pure and chaste. Bless our union with a holy love. Watch over us from Heaven. Send us grace to live in the favor of God and to share in the eternal love in which we shall all be united forever in Heaven. Amen.

Finer Femininity

Always Keep Courtship on a High Plane
(con't)

Reverent love will be a protection for both. If a boy wants the girl he goes with now to be the best wife she can be for his children; if he himself wants to be the best husband he can be for her and the best father he can be for his children, he must respect that girl before marriage.

He will do everything he can, in a positive way, and at any price, to retain or regain his personal purity and to protect the modesty and loveliness of the girl he respects, even as St. Joseph kept himself spotless and safeguarded the virginity of the Mother of God. Consequently, you need not resort to lust to enjoy one another. You will find untold happiness in the mere presence of the one you really care for—happiness which arises from the contact of mind with mind, of heart with heart, of personality with personality. This is infinitely more satisfying and enduring than mere contact of bodies.

Wondrous beauty can be found in the character of any good boy or girl if you will only patiently look for it. A young man will surely win the heart of a girl if he always acts as a gentleman and places her upon her rightful pedestal of innocence and queenly modesty. In like manner, a girl will command the respect and win the love of a boy if by words and actions she makes it clear that she will tolerate no compromise with her ideals of honor and integrity.

Any momentary weakness may be implied as an invitation to dangerous liberties. Direct your friendship so that it may square with Christ's law of honor and purity in a chaste and noble love.

Elevate your love to Christ that your love may be sweeter and more enduring. Then leaving one another, you can walk to the Communion rail and receive your Eucharistic Lord with reverent minds and chaste hearts. Where chaste love fills your company-keeping, courtship becomes an aid to virtue and an encouragement to holiness.

Always Keep Your Courtship on a High Plane

by Father Lawrence Lovasik, Clean Love in Courtship

Keep sex in the background! It must not dominate your thoughts and dictate your conduct. The physical must be subordinated to the spiritual because man is a spiritual creature and not mere animal.

Allowing your courtship to degenerate to the physical would mean a loss of honor and respect. An attraction which springs largely from the physical element of sex is an insecure foundation for enduring friendship and conjugal love.

Pure love is the foundation of a happy courtship. The reason why there are so many sinful, saddened hearts in courtship is because too many young men and women fail to distinguish clearly between love and lust; and yet they are as completely different as day is from night.

True love is pure, beautiful, noble, self-sacrificing. It is dominated by mutual respect for each other's character, not by mere emotion, passion and lust. True love is unselfish, thinking only of the good of the other; it would rather endure any self-restraint than harm the other in any way.

If love-making does not rise above the mere thrill of bodily sensations, it can be no more than indulgence in passion, which is lust. Lust, on the other hand, is ugly, base, selfish, impure; it seeks nothing outside itself. All fine promises and sweet expressions of love are but lies.

A beautiful friendship is marred because the boy and girl permit indecent liberties which are like vicious cancers eating their way into their very hearts and destroying virtue, peace and happiness.

Pure love is the best preparation for marriage; lust draws down God's curse upon it. If by company-keeping you are encouraged in purity, then true love is the basis of your friendship and enduring affection will be the result.

If through company-keeping you are encouraged to impurity, then lust, not love, is the foundation of the friendship and evil will be the result. There is a natural and necessary relationship between your conduct now and your status later in marriage.

If a young man is selfish, loose, crude, unreasonable now, do not expect that he will be unselfish, high-minded, spiritual and controlled in marriage.

The Sacraments do not change nature; they elevate it if it is disposed to be elevated. A foul love must be driven out by a fair love. In the pure love of a young man for a virtuous girl, he finds a shield against unchastity.

(Continued on following page.)

If You Want to Find the Right Person...
You Must BE the Right Person (con't)

There are so many things young ladies can be doing to make their lives full in the interim when they are waiting for Mr. Right.

Read good books. There is nothing like an inspiring book to help us make some changes that will make us a better person. Always have a book in progress that is teaching you something worthwhile.

Show more charity in your home...obedience to your parents and kindness towards your siblings. One day you will be making a home of your own. Start practicing the virtues now within your own family circle.

Learn the womanly arts. Sew, cook, crochet. So much fun...and so satisfying!! Take lessons if need be. God gave us a creative nature.....let's build on that! And you have time right now, when you are single!

Frequent the Sacraments more often. Pray, listen to sermons, do your spiritual readings. This needs to be the foundation of your life. We can busily do everything else but if we do not have the grace behind it, we are building our house on a foundation of sand.

There is so much good to be done, so much to learn and so many people to love. Your inner happiness does not have to depend on finding the right man. That happiness needs to be nurtured NOW.....and a good side benefit from that is you will be more appealing to that one good man out there that is keeping his eyes open for an excellent wife and mother of his children!

"And you, too, must stand by your convictions at the cost of things you love. An ideal is worth little if it is not worth wholehearted, honest effort. Nothing is more pitiful than a woman whose mind admires purity and right, yet whose will is too weak to choose them and whose life is blighted by sin and mire about her.
Be true, be noble, aim high, and God will give you strength to keep your ideals."
– Mabel Hale,
Beautiful Girlhood

If You Want to Find the Right Person... You Must BE the Right Person

–Mrs. Leane VanderPutten

Have you found Mr. Right yet?

If you haven't then look at it as a blessing! You still have time to become the person God has meant you to be...right where you are at. Let's face it, if you want to find Mr.Right, you need to become MISS Right first.

If you expect him to be upright, chaste, kind, loving, putting his religion first, then you need to be those things first.

Our inner happiness NOW should be a requisite for settling down into a life long relationship that will require the utmost of virtue. What are you doing to work on that each day?

I remember when I was a young lady of around 20. I had a dear friend, Kay, who was like another mother to me at the time. She asked me what my goal was in life. I told her I wanted to be a wife and a mother of a large family. She looked at me and matter-of-factly said, "Well you need to be working on that now."

I knew what she meant. I needed to roll up my sleeves, learn to become a better cook, learn the womanly arts, learn to give and to love and most important, grow in my spiritual life! Don't let any day go by without moving forward. Do not become stagnant!

You also need to rid your life of stumbling blocks that may be slowing you down in your growth of virtue.

What kind of movies are you watching? Are they the kind that you would want your potential spouse to be watching? What about your future kids? Would you want them watching those shows? Those are things we need to think about. We need to make those sacrifices NOW. God blesses these efforts a hundred fold.

Music? Ah...MUSIC! I love music just like the rest of them (ask my kids). I grew up listening to what was on the radio. Back in my day we didn't have the many choices we have nowadays. We just listened to the latest pop. In my estimation, it wasn't great.....it wasn't horrible.

There are lots of good choices out there. Clean up your act. Think about it next time....is this stuff bringing me down? Would I want my kids to be listening to it?

I'm not a stick-in-the-mud mom. I love music, I love dancing. But you had better know what NOT to listen to. There are a lot of grey areas. Pray, listen and be ready to sacrifice. We can still have fun, listen to fun music without it being displeasing to God.

What about your friends? Do they inspire you? Are they a good example? In general, are they on the same path as you? You may think that your presence in their life is going to make them a better person. Pray about that one. Oftentimes, the opposite happens and they bring us down. We need to end friendships that take us away from our goal in life....living to please God. We become like the people we associate with.

(Continued on next page..)

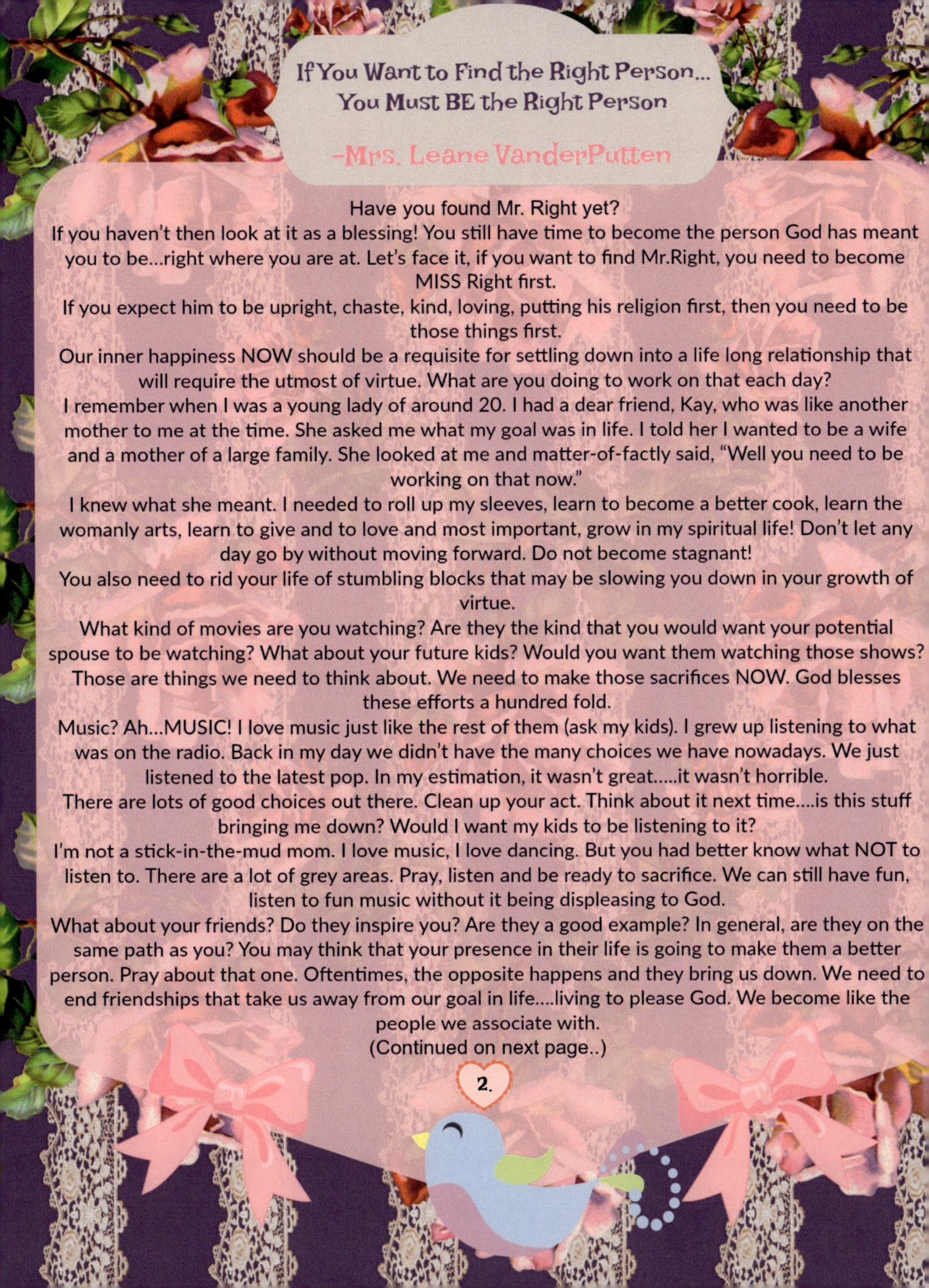

Starting Your Day....

Every morning, we may be tempted to put off our prayers until "later" or skip them altogether because we have much to do and action is where it is at.
If we allow the devil to win in this very first struggle of the day, he will win many more of the battles throughout the day.
Our Morning Prayers need to be a priority and the very foundation of our daily life.
-Finer Femininity

The MORNING is the SUNRISE of the Soul and Prayer is its first duty. Form the holy habit of raising your heart to God and let your first act be the *Sign of the Cross,* saying at the same time the words: "In the Name of the Father, and of the Son and of the Holy Ghost. Amen."

We must have a daily habit of prayer; it should be ingrained in us. Morning and Night Prayers, the Rosary and frequent lifting of the mind to God will help us to hear His Voice. The daily habit of prayer leads us to spiritual health. We are more "tuned in" to know what God's will is in our life, to desire it and to do it. By our habit of prayer we will experience the tranquility and happiness that comes from Him Who sees our efforts and loves us so much! He will give us the peace that passeth all understanding.... - Anne Joachim

THE VALUE OF THE MASS
At the hour of death the Holy Masses you have heard devoutly will be your greatest consolation.
*Every Mass will go with you to Judgment and will plead pardon for you.
*By every Mass you can diminish the temporal punishment due to your sins, according to your fervor.
*By devoutly assisting at Holy Mass you render the greatest homage possible to the Sacred Humanity of Our Lord.
*Through the Holy Sacrifice, Our Lord Jesus Christ supplies for many of your negligences and omissions.
*He forgives you all the venial sins which you are determined to avoid. He forgives you all your unknown sins which you never confessed. The Power of Satan over you is diminished.
*By piously hearing Holy Mass you afford the Souls in Purgatory the greatest possible relief.
*One Holy Mass heard during your life will be of more benefit to you than many heard for you after your death.
*Through the Holy Mass you are preserved from many dangers and misfortunes which would otherwise have befallen you. You shorten your Purgatory by every Mass.
*During Holy Mass you kneel amid a multitude of holy Angels, who are present at the Adorable Sacrifice with reverential awe.
*Through Holy Mass you are blessed in your temporal goods and affairs.
*When you hear Holy Mass devoutly, offering it to Almighty God in honor of any particular Saint or Angel thanking God for the favors bestowed on him, you afford that Saint or Angel a new degree of honor, joy and happiness, and draw his special love and protection for yourself.
*Every time you assist at Holy Mass, besides other intentions, you should offer it in honor of the Saint of the day.

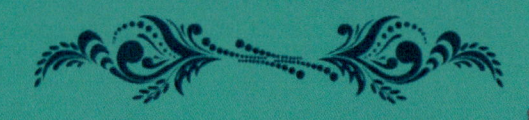

Table of Contents

Starting Your Day..page 1
If You Want to Find the Right Person.....................page 2
    (by Leane VanderPutten)
Always Keep Your Courtship on a High Plane..........page 4
    (by Father Lawrence Lovasik)
Courtship Prayer, etc...page 6
Too Young to Keep Company?................................page 7
    (by Fr. Donald Miller, C.SS.R.)
Are You Beautiful?...page 8
    (by Mabel Hale)
Dating Non-Catholics..page 10
    (by Reverend George A. Kelly)
A Tea Party..page 12
    (by Emilie Barnes)
Quotes...page 15
When is Kissing a Sin?..page 17
    (by Fr. Donald Miller)
What Do You Mean, Beauty?.................................page 18
    (by Rev. Daniel A. Lord, S.J.)
In Praise of Unmarried Women..............................page 20
    (by Rev. Daniel A. Lord, S.J.)
Frequent Confession...page 22
    (by Reverend Leo F. Griffin)
Tips for Chaste Company-Keeping........................page 24
    (by Father Lawrence Lovasik)
The Blessedness of Labor.....................................page 26
    (by Reverend George Deshon)
Single....Unpicked..page 28
    (by Leane VanderPutten)
Duties Towards Parents..page 30
    (by Father Fulgence Meyer)
What Friendship Ought to Be................................page 32
    (by Father Lasance)
Quotes...pages 34, 35
The Religious Life...page 36
    (by Father Fulgence Meyer)
Siblings...page 38
Where Are You Going?..page 39
    (by Reverend George A. Kelly)
At the End of Your Day...page 40

J.M.J.

+

Editor's Note

Dear Catholic Young Ladies,

The following pages are for you…to brighten your day, to inspire and encourage you and to help you persevere as you enter into adulthood and all that it entails.

This is a beautiful time in your life. It is also a time when many questions arise.

On these pages are articles about courting, purity, the single life, religious vocation, friends, tea parties, obedience, etc.

It won't be long until you embark on your own God-given vocation as an adult. It will be wonderful, but it will also be filled with many responsibilities. Take the time to enjoy your singleness. Live each day to its fullest….use this interval to smell the roses along the way, but also to grow spiritually and to learn the ways of a devoted Catholic woman!

May this "Maglet" (a cross between a magazine and a booklet) help and encourage you to that end, that your single days will be filled with the wholesomeness that only good Catholic living can bring!

God bless you!
Mrs. Leane VanderPutten

Acknowledgements:

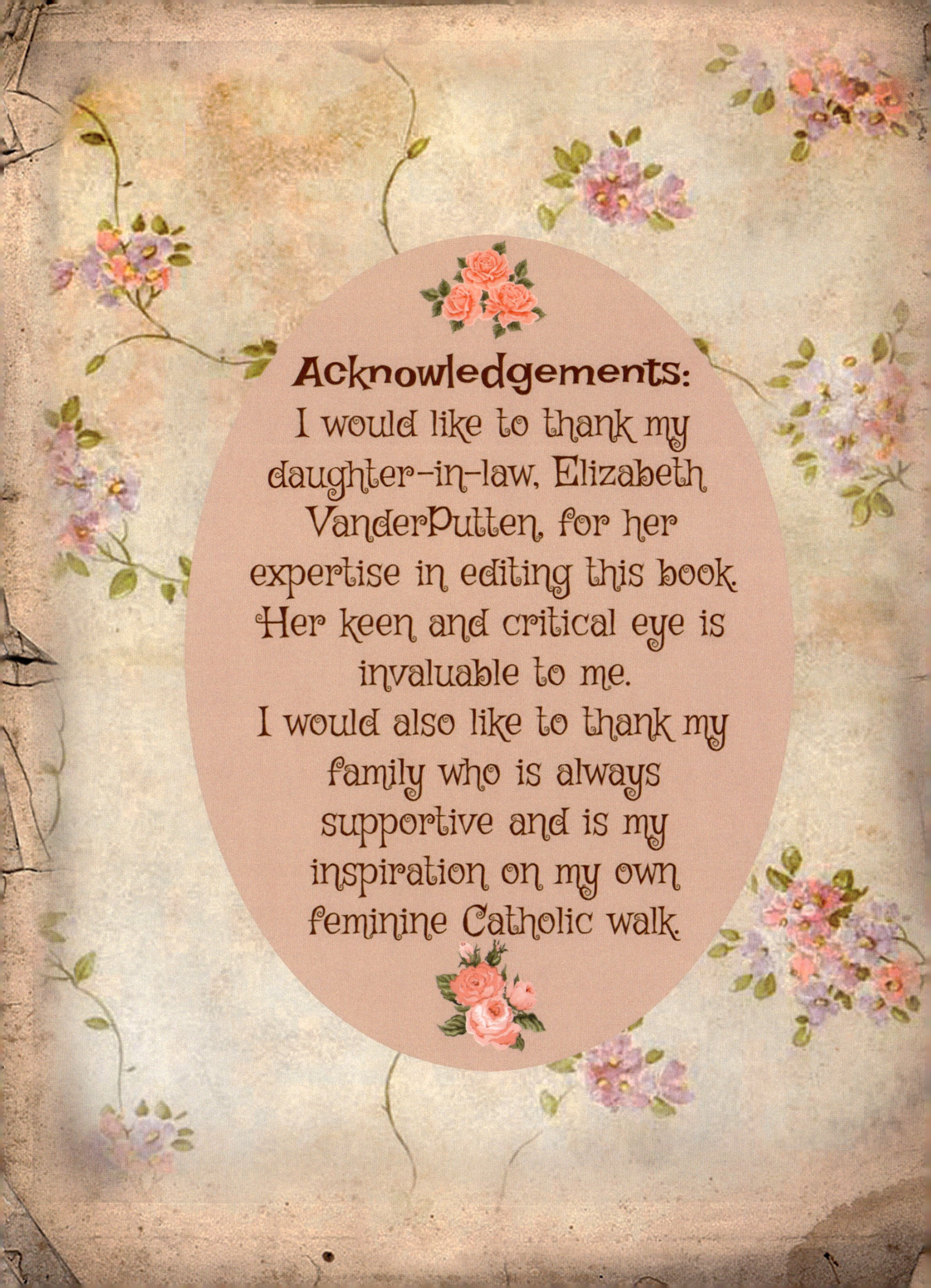

I would like to thank my daughter-in-law, Elizabeth VanderPutten, for her expertise in editing this book. Her keen and critical eye is invaluable to me.

I would also like to thank my family who is always supportive and is my inspiration on my own feminine Catholic walk.

Copyright © 2017 Leane G. VanderPutten

All rights reserved.

ISBN-13:
978-1979030557

ISBN-10:
1979030553

The Catholic Young Lady's Maglet
by Leane VanderPutten

A BEAUTIFUL RECIPE

A beautiful turning to God in prayer,
At break of day—be it dull or fair,
A beautiful word when chance occurs
Instead of the gossip which hurts and slurs;
A beautiful deed, not one or two,
But just as many as you can do;
A beautiful thought in the mind to keep
Where otherwise evil and sin might creep.
A beautiful smile—how it helps and cheers
And coaxes from others their smiles and tears;
A beautiful song in praise to Him
When the shadows fall and the lights grow dim,
If followed—you'll find it a beautiful way
To make—and so easy—a beautiful day.
From The Precious Blood and Family Prayer Book